Taste of Christmas

O Christmas Cookie

D0168320

Taste of Christmas

O Christmas Cookie

Recipes and Holiday Inspiration for Cookie Lovers

BARBOUR
PUBLISHING

A balanced diet is a
Christmas cookie in each hand!

Contents

Share these delicious Christmas cookies with family, friends, coworkers, and neighbors. Think of them as gifts from the "embassy of love." Christmas cookies inspire a precious kind of bond—from the giving to the receiving, and even the baking. A favorite cookie recipe passed down through the family has even been known to bridge the broadest generation gaps. We trust this delightful collection of holiday recipes will make your taste buds tingle, your memories—of Christmases past and present—linger, and your spirit warm with connections to the ones you hold dear in your heart.

Suddenly there was with the angel a multitude of the heavenly host praising God and saying: "Glory to God in the highest, and on earth peace, goodwill toward men!"

Luke 2:13–14

Drop Cookies

O Father, may that holy star
Grow every year more bright,
And send its glorious beams afar
To fill the world with light.

WILLIAM CULLEN BRYANT

Festive Chocolate Mint Cookies

OVEN TEMPERATURE: 350 degrees   **YIELD:** 6 dozen

¾ cup (1½ sticks) butter
1½ cups brown sugar, packed
2 tablespoons water
1 (12 ounce) bag milk chocolate chips
2 eggs

2½ cups flour
1¼ teaspoons baking soda
½ teaspoon salt
15 ounces chocolate-covered mint candies

In saucepan, combine butter, sugar, and water. Stir over low heat until butter is melted. Add chocolate chips and stir until partially melted. Remove from heat and continue to stir until chocolate chips are melted. Pour into large mixing bowl and let stand 10 minutes. With mixer on high speed, beat in eggs, one at a time. In separate bowl, sift together flour, baking soda, and salt. Add flour mixture to creamed mixture in portions, stirring until all dry ingredients are incorporated. Refrigerate dough for 1 hour. Drop by spoonfuls onto ungreased cookie sheet 1 to 2 inches apart and bake for 12 to 13 minutes. Remove from oven and place mint on each cookie. Let soften and then swirl over the top of cookie. Cool for 5 minutes before removing from pan.

Orange Drop Christmas Cookies

OVEN TEMPERATURE: 350 degrees

YIELD: 5 dozen

1 (15.25 ounce) package orange
  supreme cake mix
Grated rind of one orange
2 eggs

½ cup oil
1 (16 ounce) can cream cheese frosting
3 tablespoons red and green sprinkles

Combine cake mix, orange rind, eggs, and oil. Stir until well blended. Drop by spoonfuls onto parchment paper–lined cookie sheet 1 to 2 inches apart. Bake for 8 minutes. Cool for 5 minutes before removing from pan. Cool completely on wire rack. Top with cream cheese frosting and red and green sprinkles.

Santa's Favorite Cookies

OVEN TEMPERATURE: 350 degrees   **YIELD:** 4 dozen

1 cup sugar
1 cup light brown sugar, firmly packed
1 cup oil
2 eggs
1 teaspoon vanilla extract
1 cup cornflakes

½ cup coconut
2 cups flour
1 teaspoon baking soda
¼ teaspoon salt
½ cup pecans
½ cup oats

In large bowl, combine sugars, oil, eggs, and vanilla. Stir together. Add cornflakes and coconut. Stir well. In separate bowl, sift together flour, baking soda, and salt. Add to first mixture. Fold in pecans and oats. Drop by spoonfuls onto parchment paper–lined cookie sheet about 1 to 2 inches apart. Bake for 13 to 15 minutes. Cool for 5 minutes before removing from pan.

Happy Holiday Cookies

OVEN TEMPERATURE: 350 degrees   **YIELD:** 6 dozen

1 cup (2 sticks) butter, softened
1½ cups light brown sugar
3 eggs
3 cups flour
1 teaspoon baking soda
1 pound dates, chopped

1 pound walnuts, chopped
½ pound golden raisins
½ cup apple juice
1 (16 ounce) jar maraschino cherries,
  drained and cut in half

In large bowl, cream butter and sugar. Add eggs. Beat until ingredients are combined. In separate bowl, sift together flour and baking soda. Add to creamed mixture in portions, stirring until all dry ingredients are well incorporated. Fold in dates, walnuts, raisins, and apple juice. Drop by spoonfuls 1 inch apart onto ungreased cookie sheet. Top each with cherry halves. Bake for 10 to 12 minutes. Cool for 5 minutes before removing from pan.

Holiday Fruit and Spice Cookies

OVEN TEMPERATURE: 325 degrees

YIELD: 6 dozen

1 cup (2 sticks) butter, softened
1½ cups sugar
3 eggs, beaten
3 cups flour
1 tablespoon cocoa powder
1 teaspoon nutmeg
1 teaspoon mace
1 teaspoon cinnamon
½ teaspoon ginger
½ teaspoon allspice

¾ teaspoon baking soda
1 tablespoon liquid coffee
½ cup candied cherries, chopped
½ cup candied pineapple, chopped
⅓ cup dates, chopped
¼ cup candied orange peel, chopped
¼ cup flour
½ cup currants
1 cup white raisins
1 pound mixed nuts, chopped

In large bowl, cream butter and sugar until fluffy. Add eggs and beat well. In separate bowl, sift together flour, cocoa, spices, and baking soda. Add to creamed mixture. Add coffee. Mix well. Toss cherries, pineapple, dates, and orange peel in ¼ cup flour until coated and add to creamed mixture. Fold in currants, raisins, and nuts. Drop by spoonfuls onto greased cookie sheet. Bake for 12 to 15 minutes. Cookies should be crisp with a rich color, but not brown. Cool for 5 minutes before removing from pan.

Christmas Fruties

OVEN TEMPERATURE: 375 degrees

YIELD: 3 dozen

1 cup pecans, coarsely chopped
1 cup dates, coarsely chopped
¼ cup milk
1 teaspoon cider vinegar
1 cup candied red and green cherries,
   coarsely chopped
¼ cup flour

½ cup (1 stick) butter, softened
¾ cup brown sugar
1 egg
2 teaspoons lemon rind
1 cup flour
½ teaspoon baking soda
½ teaspoon salt

Combine pecans, dates, milk, and cider vinegar. Coat cherries in flour and add to first mixture. Let stand 10 minutes. In large bowl, cream butter with sugar. Add egg and stir well. Add lemon rind. Stir and set aside. Sift together flour, baking soda, and salt. Stir flour mixture into creamed mixture until dry ingredients are incorporated. Fold in fruit and nuts. Drop by spoonfuls onto ungreased cookie sheet. Bake for 10 to 12 minutes. Cool for 5 minutes before removing from pan.

Gumdrop Marvels

OVEN TEMPERATURE: 375 degrees

YIELD: 3 dozen

1 cup shortening
1 cup sugar
1 cup brown sugar
2 eggs
1 teaspoon vanilla extract
2 cups flour

1 teaspoon baking powder
½ teaspoon salt
2 cups oats
1 cup coconut
1 cup gumdrops, chopped

In large bowl, cream shortening and sugars. Add eggs and beat until fluffy. Stir in vanilla. In separate bowl, sift together flour, baking powder, baking soda, and salt. Add to creamed mixture. Add oats, coconut, and gumdrops. Stir well. Drop by spoonfuls onto greased cookie sheet and press with fork. Bake for 10 minutes. Cool for 5 minutes before removing from pan.

Fig Chewies

OVEN TEMPERATURE: 375 degrees

YIELD: 4 dozen

1 cup dried figs, chopped
½ cup water
1 cup shortening
1 cup brown sugar, firmly packed
1 egg

1 teaspoon vanilla extract
1¾ cups flour
2 teaspoons baking powder
¾ teaspoon salt
1⅓ cups flaked coconut

In saucepan, combine figs and water. Bring to boil over *medium* heat. Cook and stir until figs are tender (about 5 minutes). Cool. In large bowl, cream shortening and sugar until fluffy. Add egg and vanilla. Beat well. Add figs and mix well. In separate bowl, sift together flour, baking powder, and salt. Add flour in small amounts, stirring well after each portion. Take spoonful of dough and roll into 1-inch ball. Roll in coconut and place onto greased cookie sheet. Bake for 15 to 18 minutes. Cool for 5 minutes before removing from pan.

Tutti-Frutti Cookies

OVEN TEMPERATURE: 400 degrees

YIELD: 5 dozen

¾ cup maraschino cherries, chopped
¾ cup candied pineapple, chopped
2 tablespoons candied orange peel, chopped
2½ teaspoons rum extract
¾ cup (1½ sticks) butter, softened
½ cup brown sugar, firmly packed
2 eggs, unbeaten

¾ cup walnuts, chopped
1¾ cups cake flour
1 teaspoon baking powder
½ teaspoon cinnamon
⅛ teaspoon cloves
¼ teaspoon salt
¼ cup milk

Combine cherries, pineapple, orange peel, and rum extract. Place in tightly covered jar for 24 hours, stirring occasionally. In large bowl, cream butter with sugar until fluffy. Add eggs, one at a time, beating thoroughly after each. Add fruit mixture and walnuts. Mix well. In separate bowl, sift together flour, baking powder, spices, and salt. Add flour and milk alternately in small amounts, stirring well after each addition. Drop by spoonfuls onto greased cookie sheet. Bake for 10 minutes. Cool for 5 minutes before removing from pan.

Rudolph's Ranger Cookies

OVEN TEMPERATURE: 350 degrees   **YIELD:** 5 dozen

1 cup shortening
1 cup sugar
1 cup light brown sugar, firmly packed
2 eggs
1 teaspoon vanilla extract
2 cups flour
1 teaspoon baking powder

1 teaspoon baking soda
¼ teaspoon salt
2 cups oats
2 cups rice cereal
1 cup coconut
1 cup nuts

In large bowl, cream shortening and sugars. Add eggs, one at a time, stirring well after each addition. Stir in vanilla. In separate bowl, sift together flour, baking powder, baking soda, and salt. Add flour mixture to sugar mixture and mix well. Add oats, rice cereal, coconut, and nuts. Combine well. Chill dough for 1 hour. Take one spoonful of dough at a time and roll it into a ball. Place on greased cookie sheet. Flatten each with fork. Bake for 25 minutes. Cool for 5 minutes before removing from pan.

Cherry Kisses

OVEN TEMPERATURE: 350 degrees

YIELD: 4 dozen

4 egg whites
1 teaspoon salt
1¼ cups sugar

1 teaspoon vanilla extract
2 cups flaked coconut
24 maraschino cherries, cut in half

Combine egg whites and salt in large bowl and beat with electric mixer on *high* until firm peaks appear. Add sugar, 1 tablespoon at a time, beating after each addition. Add vanilla and coconut, mixing lightly. Drop by spoonfuls onto ungreased cookie sheet. Bake for 20 minutes. Cool for 5 minutes before removing from pan. Top each with a cherry half.

Mrs. Santa's Molasses Cookies

OVEN TEMPERATURE: 400 degrees   **YIELD:** 3 dozen

½ cup shortening
1 cup sugar
1 egg, unbeaten
½ cup molasses
3 cups flour
1½ teaspoons baking soda

½ teaspoon salt
1 teaspoon ginger
1½ teaspoons cinnamon
1 cup buttermilk
½ teaspoon vanilla extract

In large bowl, cream shortening with sugar until fluffy. Add egg and beat well. Add molasses. Mix well. In separate bowl, sift together flour, baking soda, salt, and spices. In a cup, stir together buttermilk and vanilla. Add flour alternately with buttermilk, in small amounts, mixing well after each addition. Refrigerate for 2 hours. Drop spoonfuls about 2 inches apart on greased cookie sheet. Bake for 10 to 12 minutes. Cool for 5 minutes before removing from pan.

Christmas Kisses

OVEN TEMPERATURE: 350 degrees   **YIELD:** 3 dozen

2 egg whites
¼ teaspoon salt
1 cup sugar

1 teaspoon grated orange rind
3 cups cornflakes cereal

Combine egg whites with salt and beat with electric mixer on *low* until foamy. Add sugar, 2 tablespoons at a time, beating on *low* after each addition. On *high*, beat until standing peaks are formed. Fold in orange rind. Add cereal and stir until incorporated. Drop by spoonfuls onto greased cookie sheet. Bake for 15 minutes. Cool for 5 minutes before removing from pan.

Roly-Poly Snowballs

OVEN TEMPERATURE: 300 degrees

YIELD: 4 dozen

1 cup (2 sticks) butter, softened
¼ cup sugar
2 cups flour, sifted

2 cups pecans, chopped
1½ cups powdered sugar

In large bowl, cream butter with sugar. Add flour. Mix until well incorporated. Fold in pecans. Take spoonfuls of dough and roll into 1-inch balls. Bake for 45 minutes. Cool for 5 minutes before removing from pan. As soon as they can be handled, roll cookies in powdered sugar. When they have cooled thoroughly, roll in sugar a second time.

Cherry Winks

OVEN TEMPERATURE: 375 degrees

YIELD: 3 dozen

¾ cup shortening
1 cup sugar
2 eggs
2 tablespoons milk
1 teaspoon vanilla extract
2¼ cups flour
1 teaspoon baking powder

½ teaspoon baking soda
½ teaspoon salt
1 cup pecans, chopped
1 cup dates, chopped
2½ cups cornflake cereal
⅓ cup maraschino cherries, cut into quarters

In large bowl, cream shortening with sugar until fluffy. Add eggs, one at a time, stirring after each. Add milk and vanilla. Mix well. In separate bowl, sift together flour, baking powder, baking soda, and salt. Add flour mixture in small portions, stirring after each addition. Fold in pecans and dates. Mix well. Crush cornflakes in a bowl. Take spoonfuls of dough and roll into 1-inch balls. Then roll dough balls in cornflake crumbs. Place on greased cookie sheet about 1 to 2 inches apart. Place one cherry piece on each cookie. Bake for 10 to 12 minutes. Cool for 5 minutes before removing from pan.

Santa's Chocolate Pixies

OVEN TEMPERATURE: 350 degrees

YIELD: 3 dozen

¼ cup (½ stick) butter
4 (1 ounce) squares semisweet or milk chocolate
2 cups sugar
4 eggs

2 cups flour
2 teaspoons baking powder
½ teaspoon salt
½ cup walnuts
1 cup powdered sugar

In saucepan, melt butter with chocolate over *low* heat until smooth. Remove from heat and cool. Blend in sugar and eggs, one at a time, blending well after each. In large bowl, sift together flour, baking powder, and salt. Add chocolate mixture to flour mixture and stir until all dry ingredients are incorporated. Fold in walnuts. Refrigerate dough for 1 hour. Take spoonfuls of dough and roll into 1-inch balls. Roll balls in powdered sugar. Place on greased cookie sheet about 1 to 2 inches apart. Bake for 20 minutes. Cool for 5 minutes before removing from pan.

German Chocolate Cookies

OVEN TEMPERATURE: 350 degrees

YIELD: 5 dozen

1 (15.25 ounce) package German chocolate cake mix
2 eggs
½ cup (1 stick) butter, melted

¾ cup oats
1 (6 ounce) bag semisweet chocolate chips
½ cup pecans, chopped

Beat cake mix, eggs, and butter with electric mixer on *medium*. Add oats. Stir well. Fold in chocolate chips and pecans. Place by spoonfuls on ungreased cookie sheet. Bake for 8 to 10 minutes. Cool for 5 minutes before removing from pan.

Reindeer Chip Cookies

OVEN TEMPERATURE: 350 degrees

YIELD: 6 dozen

1 cup (2 sticks) butter, softened
1 cup shortening
2 cups light brown sugar
2 cups sugar
4 eggs
2 teaspoons vanilla extract
4 cups flour
2 teaspoons baking powder
2 teaspoons baking soda

1 (12 ounce) package semisweet chocolate chips
1 (12 ounce) package peanut butter chips
2 cups oats
2 cups crispy rice cereal
1 cup flaked coconut
1 cup pecans, chopped

In large bowl, cream together butter, shortening, sugars, eggs, and vanilla. In separate bowl, sift together flour, baking powder, and baking soda. Stir into creamed mixture until well blended. Add chocolate chips, peanut butter chips, oats, rice cereal, coconut, and pecans. Stir until well incorporated. Drop by spoonfuls onto ungreased cookie sheet. Bake for 13 to 20 minutes. Let cool 5 minutes before removing from pan.

'Tis the Season Oats Yummies

OVEN TEMPERATURE: 375 degrees   **YIELD:** 6 dozen

1¼ cups (2½ sticks) butter, softened
¾ cup light brown sugar, firmly packed
½ cup sugar
1 egg
1 teaspoon vanilla extract
1½ cups flour

1 teaspoon baking soda
1 teaspoon salt
3 cups oats
1 (12 ounce) package semisweet
   chocolate chips

In large bowl, cream butter with sugars until fluffy. Beat in egg and vanilla. In separate bowl, sift together flour, baking soda, and salt. Add to creamed mixture and stir until blended. Stir in oats. Stir in chocolate chips. Drop by spoonfuls onto ungreased cookie sheets. Bake 9 to 11 minutes. Cool for 5 minutes before removing from pan.

Gerry's Deluxe Christmas Cookies

OVEN TEMPERATURE: 375 degrees

YIELD: 6 dozen

1 cup (2 sticks) butter, softened
1½ cups peanut butter
2 cups sugar
2 cups light brown sugar
6 eggs
2 tablespoons corn syrup

4 teaspoons baking soda
½ teaspoon salt
9 cups oats
1 (16 ounce) package chocolate chips
1 cup chocolate-covered candies

In large bowl, cream butter and peanut butter with sugars. Add eggs, two at a time, stirring well after each. Add corn syrup. Stir well. Add baking soda and salt. Mix well. Stir in oats, chocolate chips, and chocolate-covered candies. Stir until well blended. Drop by spoonfuls onto greased cookie sheet. Use your finger to pat down tops of cookies. Bake for 8 to 10 minutes. Cool for 5 minutes before removing from pan.

Sesame Seed Cookies

OVEN TEMPERATURE: 375 degrees

YIELD: 3 dozen

½ cup (1 stick) plus 1 tablespoon
   butter, softened
1 cup plus 2 tablespoons sugar
2 eggs, beaten
2¾ cups wheat flour

3 tablespoons milk
⅔ cup raisins
⅔ cup sesame seeds
½ teaspoon nutmeg

In medium bowl, cream butter with sugar until fluffy. Stir in eggs, one at a time, stirring after each. Add flour alternately with milk. Stir well. Add raisins, sesame seeds, and nutmeg. Stir until evenly distributed. Drop by spoonfuls onto greased cookie sheets. Flatten slightly with bottom of spoon. Bake for 10 to 15 minutes. Cool for 5 minutes before removing from pan.

Nina's Chocolate Christmas Cookies

OVEN TEMPERATURE: 350 degrees   **YIELD:** 6 dozen

1½ cups shortening
2 cups sugar
4 eggs
1 cup strong liquid coffee
2 teaspoons vanilla extract
1 teaspoon grated orange rind
5 cups flour
6 teaspoons baking powder

½ cup cocoa powder
2 teaspoons cinnamon
2 teaspoons cloves
1 cup walnuts, chopped
3 tablespoons milk
¾ teaspoon vanilla extract
1½ teaspoons lemon extract
1¼ cups powdered sugar

In large bowl, cream shortening with sugar. Add eggs, one at a time, stirring after each. Add coffee, vanilla, and orange rind. Stir well. In separate bowl, sift together flour, baking powder, cocoa, and spices. Incorporate into creamed mixture. Fold in walnuts. Take dough by spoonfuls and shape into 1-inch balls. Place on ungreased cookie sheets and bake for 15 minutes. Cool for 5 minutes before removing from pan. Combine milk with vanilla and lemon extracts. Stir slightly. Add enough sugar to make desired consistency. Frost cookies while still warm.

Santa's Soft Chocolate Cookies

OVEN TEMPERATURE: 350 degrees

YIELD: 5 dozen

½ cup shortening
1 cup light brown sugar, packed
1 egg
1 teaspoon vanilla extract
1⅓ cups flour
2 tablespoons cocoa powder
½ teaspoon baking soda

⅛ teaspoon salt
½ cup milk
½ cup (1 stick) butter, softened
2 cups powdered sugar
1 teaspoon vanilla extract
Red and green food coloring

In large bowl, cream shortening with sugar. Add egg and vanilla. Stir well. In separate bowl, sift together flour, cocoa, baking soda, and salt. Add flour mixture to creamed mixture alternately with milk. Stir well. Bake for 8 minutes. Cool for 5 minutes before removing from pan. For frosting, cream butter with powdered sugar. Add vanilla. Divide into 2 parts. Add green food coloring to one. Add red food coloring to the other. When cookies are cooled completely, frost half of them with each, covering middle of cookies only.

Bird's Nests

OVEN TEMPERATURE: 375 degrees

YIELD: 30 to 35 cookies

½ cup (1 stick) butter, softened
¼ cup light brown sugar
1 egg yolk
½ teaspoon vanilla extract
1 cup flour

¼ teaspoon salt
1 egg white, slightly beaten
1 cup pecans or walnuts, finely
  chopped
⅓ cup strawberry whole fruit preserves

In large bowl, cream together butter with sugar. Add egg yolk and vanilla. Stir well. In separate bowl, sift together flour and salt. Add to creamed mixture and blend well. Take dough by spoonfuls and roll into 1-inch balls. Dip each into egg white. Roll balls in nuts and place on ungreased cookie sheets. Bake for 5 minutes. (Watch carefully as they tend to burn easily.) Remove from oven and use thimble to make hole in center of each cookie. Return to oven and bake for 6 minutes. Cool for 5 minutes before removing from pan to wire rack. When completely cooled, add strawberry preserves to centers.

Chocolate Crinkles

OVEN TEMPERATURE: 350 degrees

YIELD: 3 dozen

½ cup vegetable oil
2 cups sugar
4 eggs
4 (1 ounce) squares unsweetened
    chocolate, melted

2 teaspoons vanilla extract
2 cups flour
2 teaspoons baking powder
½ teaspoon salt
½ cup powdered sugar, sifted

In large bowl, mix together oil and sugar. Blend in eggs, one at a time, stirring after each. Add melted chocolate and vanilla. Set aside. In separate bowl, sift together flour, baking powder, and salt. Add to chocolate mixture in small portions. Stir into soft cookie dough. Cover and refrigerate overnight. Take spoonfuls of dough and roll into 1-inch balls. Roll balls in powdered sugar and place 1 to 2 inches apart on ungreased cookie sheets. Bake for 10 minutes. Cool for 5 minutes before removing from pan.

Holiday Snackers

OVEN TEMPERATURE: 375 degrees   **YIELD:** 6 dozen

1 cup (2 sticks) butter, softened
1 cup light brown sugar, firmly packed
½ cup sugar
2 eggs
2 teaspoons vanilla extract
2¼ cups flour
1 teaspoon baking soda

1 teaspoon salt
1 cup red and green candy-coated
   chocolates
1 (6 ounce) package mini semisweet
   chocolate chips
1 cup pecans or walnuts, chopped

In large bowl, cream butter with sugars. Add eggs and mix well. Stir in vanilla. In separate bowl, sift together flour, baking soda, and salt. Add in portions to creamed mixture. Add candies, chocolate chips, and nuts. Stir until evenly blended. Drop by spoonfuls onto ungreased cookie sheets. Bake for 10 to 12 minutes. Cool for 5 minutes before removing from pan.

Ho-Ho Holiday Cookies

OVEN TEMPERATURE: 375 degrees

YIELD: 9 dozen

5 cups oats
2 cups (4 sticks) butter, softened
2 cups sugar
2 cups light brown sugar, firmly
 packed
4 eggs
2 teaspoons vanilla extract

4 cups flour
2 teaspoons baking powder
2 teaspoons baking soda
1 teaspoon salt
3 cups chocolate chips
1 (8 ounce) chocolate bar, grated
3 cups mixed nuts, chopped

In blender or food processor, reduce oats to a fine volume. Set aside. In large bowl, cream butter with sugars. Add eggs, one at a time, stirring well after each. Add vanilla. In separate bowl, sift together flour, baking powder, baking soda, and salt. Stir oats into flour mixture. Add flour mixture to creamed mixture and stir until well blended. Add chocolate chips, grated candy bar, and nuts. Stir until evenly distributed. Pinch off spoonfuls of dough and roll into 1½-inch balls and place 3 inches apart on ungreased cookie sheets. Bake for 6 minutes. Cool for 5 minutes before removing from pan.

Cream Cheese Christmas Delights

OVEN TEMPERATURE: 350 degrees

YIELD: 4 dozen

1 cup (2 sticks) butter, softened
½ (8 ounce) package cream cheese,
   softened
1 cup sugar

1 egg yolk
1 teaspoon vanilla extract
2½ cups flour, sifted
½ cup Red Hots

Cream together butter, cream cheese, and sugar. Add egg yolk and vanilla. Stir well. Add flour and stir until well blended. Drop by spoonfuls onto ungreased cookie sheet 1 to 2 inches apart. Add candies to top of each cookie. Bake for 10 to 15 minutes. Cookies should be set but not brown. Cool for 5 minutes before removing from pan.

Fruit Drop Christmas Cookies

OVEN TEMPERATURE: 400 degrees

YIELD: 8 dozen

1 cup shortening, softened
2 cups light brown sugar, firmly
   packed
2 eggs
½ cup buttermilk
3½ cups flour

1 teaspoon baking soda
1 teaspoon salt
1½ cups pecan pieces
2 cups candied cherries, cut in halves
2 cups dates, chopped

In large bowl, cream together shortening and sugar. Add eggs, one at a time, stirring well after each. Add buttermilk and stir well. In separate bowl, sift flour, baking soda, and salt. Stir into creamed mixture in portions. Fold in pecans, cherries, and dates until evenly distributed. Cover and refrigerate for 1 hour. When chilled, drop by spoonfuls onto lightly greased cookie sheet 1 to 2 inches apart. Bake for 8 to 10 minutes. Cool for 5 minutes before removing from pan.

Innkeeper's Ginger Cookies

OVEN TEMPERATURE: 375 degrees   **YIELD:** 3 dozen

¾ cup shortening
1 cup sugar
1 egg
¼ cup molasses
2 cups flour
2 teaspoons baking soda

¼ teaspoon salt
1 teaspoon cinnamon
1 teaspoon cloves
1 teaspoon ginger
1 cup sugar crystals

In large bowl, cream shortening with sugar. Add egg and molasses. Stir well. In separate bowl, sift together flour, baking soda, salt, and spices. Add to creamed mixture in portions until all dry ingredients are well incorporated. Cover dough and refrigerate for 1 hour. Take spoonfuls of dough and roll into 1-inch balls. Roll in sugar and place on ungreased cookie sheets 1 to 2 inches apart. Bake for 8 to 10 minutes. Cool for 5 minutes before removing from pan.

Grandma's Buttermilk Sugar Cookies

OVEN TEMPERATURE: 400 degrees

YIELD: 3 dozen

½ cup shortening
1½ cups sugar
2 eggs
2½ cups flour
1 teaspoon baking powder

½ teaspoon baking soda
½ teaspoon salt
½ cup buttermilk
1 teaspoon lemon extract
1 teaspoon vanilla extract

In large bowl, cream together shortening and sugar. Beat in eggs, one at a time, stirring well after each. In separate bowl, sift together flour, baking powder, baking soda, and salt. Combine buttermilk and both extracts. Add buttermilk mixture to creamed mixture, alternating with flour mixture until all dry ingredients are well incorporated. Drop by spoonfuls onto ungreased cookie sheet 1 to 2 inches apart. Bake for 8 to 10 minutes or until golden brown. Cool for 5 minutes before removing from pan.

Heavenly Delights

OVEN TEMPERATURE: 350 degrees   **YIELD:** 3½ dozen

½ cup (1 stick) butter, softened
½ cup shortening
⅔ cup powdered sugar, sifted
1 teaspoon vanilla extract

1 teaspoon orange extract
2 cups flour
½ cup pecans, chopped
1 cup powdered sugar

Cream butter and shortening; gradually add powdered sugar and extracts, beating until fluffy. Add flour gradually, beating well. Stir in pecans. Take spoonfuls of dough and shape into 1-inch balls. Place on cookie sheets 1 to 2 inches apart. Bake for 20 minutes. Cool for 5 minutes. Remove from cookie sheets and roll in powdered sugar. Cool completely. Roll in sugar a second time.

Christmas Doodles

OVEN TEMPERATURE: 375 degrees

YIELD: 3 dozen

1 cup (2 sticks) butter, softened
1½ cups sugar
2 eggs
1 teaspoon vanilla extract
2¾ cups flour

2 teaspoons cream of tartar
1 teaspoon baking soda
½ teaspoon salt
Red and green sugar crystals
Cinnamon

In large bowl, cream butter with sugar. Add eggs and vanilla; mix well. Sift together flour, cream of tartar, baking soda, and salt. Add to creamed mixture and stir until dry ingredients are fully incorporated. Cover and refrigerate dough for 30 minutes. Take by spoonfuls and roll into 1-inch balls. Roll balls in sugar crystals and cinnamon. Place on ungreased cookie sheets 1 to 2 inches apart. Bake for 8 to 10 minutes. Cool for 5 minutes before removing from pan.

Peanut Butter Oats Cookies

OVEN TEMPERATURE: 375 degrees

YIELD: 5 dozen

½ cup shortening
½ cup peanut butter
½ cup light brown sugar
1 egg
¼ cup milk

1 cup sugar
½ teaspoon baking soda
¼ teaspoon salt
2½ cups oats
½ cup raisins

In large bowl, cream shortening with peanut butter and brown sugar. Mix together egg and milk and add to creamed mixture. In separate bowl, sift together sugar, baking soda, and salt. Incorporate into creamed mixture. Add oats in small portions, blending after each addition. Stir in raisins. Drop by spoonfuls onto ungreased cookie sheets 2 inches apart. Bake 10 to 12 minutes.

Bar Cookies

When we recall Christmas past, we usually find that
the simplest things—not the great occasions—give off
the greatest glow of happiness.

BOB HOPE

Bethlehem Bars

OVEN TEMPERATURE: 350 degrees   **YIELD:** 15 servings

¾ cup butter, melted
1 cup flour
1 cup oats
¾ cup light brown sugar, firmly packed
1 teaspoon baking soda

32 caramels, unwrapped
1 tablespoon butter
3 tablespoons milk
½ cup nuts, chopped
1 cup chocolate chips

In large bowl, combine butter, flour, oats, sugar, and baking soda. Press about ¾ of mixture into bottom of greased 11 x 9 x 2–inch pan. Bake for 10 to 12 minutes. Cool on wire rack. In saucepan, combine caramels, butter, and milk. Stir constantly until all are melted. Pour over baked crust and sprinkle nuts and chocolate chips over top. Add remaining oats mixture and bake for an additional 15 minutes.

Spicy Pecan Squares

OVEN TEMPERATURE: 350 degrees   **YIELD:** 15 squares

1 cup (2 sticks) butter
1 cup light brown sugar, firmly packed
1 egg, separated
1 teaspoon vanilla extract

2 cups flour
½ teaspoon salt
1 teaspoon cinnamon
1 cup pecans, finely chopped

In large bowl, cream butter with sugar. Add egg and vanilla, and beat until fluffy. In separate bowl, sift together flour, salt, and cinnamon. Add flour mixture and half the pecans. Mix well. Press into greased 13 x 11 x 2–inch baking pan. Sprinkle with remaining nuts. Bake for 25 to 30 minutes. Cool before cutting into bars.

Grandma's Frosty Strawberry Squares

OVEN TEMPERATURE: 350 degrees

YIELD: 12 to 14 squares

1 cup flour
¼ cup brown sugar
½ cup nuts, chopped
½ cup (1 stick) butter, melted
2 egg whites

1 cup sugar
2 cups fresh strawberries, sliced
2 tablespoons lemon juice
1 cup whipping cream

Stir together flour, sugar, nuts, and butter. Spread mixture in 13 x 9 x 2–inch pan and bake for 20 minutes, stirring occasionally to make crumbs. Remove ⅓ cup of crumbs from pan and cool. In large bowl, combine egg whites, sugar, strawberries, and lemon juice. Beat at *high* speed until stiff peaks are formed (10 minutes). Whip cream and fold into strawberry mixture. Spoon over crumbs and top with reserved crumb mixture. Freeze overnight. Cut into squares.

Turtle Brownies

OVEN TEMPERATURE: 350 degrees

YIELD: 36 squares

1 (14 ounce) package caramels
1 (5 ounce) can sweetened condensed milk, divided
1 (15.25 ounce) German chocolate cake mix

¾ cup (1½ sticks) butter, melted
1 cup pecans, chopped
1 (6 ounce) package semiswcet chocolate chips

In saucepan, melt caramels with ⅓ cup sweetened condensed milk. Mix together cake mix, butter, remainder of milk, and pecans. Press half of cake mixture into greased 13 x 9 x 2–inch pan. Bake for 6 minutes. Take out of oven and immediately pour chocolate chips evenly over cake layer. Drizzle caramel over chocolate chips. Press remainder of cake mixture on top. Bake for 16 minutes. Cool before cutting into small squares.

Cinnamon Crunch Bars

OVEN TEMPERATURE: 350 degrees

YIELD: 30 bars

1 cup (2 sticks) butter, softened
1½ cups light brown sugar, firmly packed
½ cup sugar
2 eggs
2 teaspoons vanilla extract
1 teaspoon grated orange peel

1¾ cups flour
1 teaspoon baking soda
1 teaspoon salt
1 teaspoon cinnamon
1 cup milk chocolate chips
1 cup white chocolate chips

In large bowl, cream butter with sugars until fluffy. Add eggs, one at a time, beating well after each. Add vanilla and orange peel. Beat well. In separate bowl, sift together flour, baking soda, salt, and cinnamon. Stir into creamed mixture. Stir in chocolate chips. Turn batter into greased 13 x 9 x 2–inch baking pan. Bake for 25 to 35 minutes. Cool completely in pan before cutting into bars.

Chocolate Banana Bars

OVEN TEMPERATURE: 350 degrees

YIELD: 14 bars

½ cup (1 stick) butter, softened
1 cup sugar
1 egg
1 teaspoon vanilla extract
5 ripe bananas, mashed
1½ cups flour

¼ cup cocoa powder
1 teaspoon baking powder
1 teaspoon baking soda
½ teaspoon salt
½ cup walnuts, chopped

In large bowl, cream butter with sugar until creamy. Add egg and vanilla. Beat until fluffy. Add bananas. Stir well. In separate bowl, sift together flour, cocoa powder, baking powder, baking soda, and salt. Add in portions to creamed mixture, stirring until all dry ingredients are incorporated. Add walnuts and stir until well distributed. Turn batter into greased 13 x 9 x 2–inch baking pan. Bake for 30 to 35 minutes. Cool completely before cutting into squares.

Brickle Bars

OVEN TEMPERATURE: 350 degrees

YIELD: 16 bars

½ cup (1 stick) butter
4 (1 ounce) squares unsweetened
  chocolate
1 cup sugar
2 eggs

1 teaspoon vanilla extract
¾ cup flour
½ cup miniature semisweet chocolate
  chips
¾ cup almond brickle pieces

In large saucepan, stir together butter and chocolate over *low* heat until melted.
Remove from heat and stir in sugar. Add eggs and vanilla, mixing lightly just
until combined. *Do not overmix.* Add flour using as few strokes as possible
to incorporate. Spread batter in 8 x 8 x 2–inch baking pan. Sprinkle with
chocolate chips and almond brickle pieces. Bake for 30 minutes. Cool before
cutting into squares.

Apple Brown Betty Bars

OVEN TEMPERATURE: 375 degrees

YIELD: 3 dozen

1½ cups flour
1 teaspoon baking soda
1 teaspoon salt
½ cup nuts, chopped
1½ cups quick oats
1½ cups light brown sugar,
  firmly packed

1 cup shortening, melted
2½ cups apple slices
2 tablespoons butter
½ cup sugar

Sift together flour, baking soda, and salt. Add nuts, oats, and brown sugar. Add melted shortening and mix until crumbly. Press half the dough into 11 x 9 x 2–inch baking pan. Place apple slices over dough. Dot with butter and sprinkle with sugar. Add second half of dough over apple slices and pat down. Bake for 25 to 35 minutes. Cool in pan before cutting into squares.

Chocolaty Cream Cheese Bars

OVEN TEMPERATURE: 350 degrees　　**YIELD:** 24 bars

5 tablespoons butter, softened
⅓ cup sugar
⅓ cup light brown sugar, firmly packed
1 egg
1 egg yolk
1 teaspoon vanilla extract
1½ cups flour

¾ teaspoon baking soda
¾ cup semisweet chocolate chips
1 (8 ounce) package cream cheese, softened
¼ cup sugar
1 egg
½ teaspoon vanilla extract

In large bowl, cream butter with sugars. Add egg, egg yolk, and vanilla. Beat well. In separate bowl, sift together flour and baking soda. Add flour mixture to creamed mixture and stir until all dry ingredients are incorporated. Add chocolate chips. Reserve 1 cup of dough. Press remaining dough into bottom of lightly greased 8 x 8 x 2–inch baking pan. Bake for 10 minutes. Cream cream cheese with sugar. Beat in egg and vanilla. Spread over crust. Sprinkle reserved dough over top. Bake for 18 minutes. Cool on wire rack. Cover and refrigerate for 1 hour before cutting.

Yummy Toffee Bars

OVEN TEMPERATURE: 350 degrees

YIELD: 4 dozen bars

1½ cups (3 sticks) butter, softened
1¾ cups light brown sugar, firmly
   packed
2 teaspoons vanilla extract

3 cups flour, sifted
1 (16 ounce) package milk chocolate
   chips

In large bowl, cream butter with sugar. Add vanilla and stir until well blended.
Add flour and stir until well incorporated. Stir in half of the chocolate chips.
Spread dough in greased 13 x 9 x 2–inch baking pan. Bake for 22 minutes.
While still hot, sprinkle remaining chocolate chips over top of baked cookie.
As they melt, spread evenly over top. Before cutting, cool until chocolate on
top is set.

Delicate Lemon Squares

OVEN TEMPERATURE: 350 degrees

YIELD: 3 dozen

1 cup flour
¼ cup powdered sugar
½ cup (1 stick) butter, softened
2 eggs, beaten
1 cup sugar

½ teaspoon grated lemon rind
2 tablespoons lemon juice
2 tablespoons flour
½ teaspoon baking powder
2 tablespoons powdered sugar, sifted

In medium bowl, combine 1 cup flour and powdered sugar. Cut in butter with pastry blender until mixture resembles coarse meal. Press mixture evenly in ungreased 9 x 9 x 2–inch baking pan. Bake for 15 minutes. Combine eggs, sugar, lemon rind, and lemon juice. Beat well. Combine 2 tablespoons flour and baking powder and stir into egg mixture. Pour over baked crust. Bake for 20 minutes or until lightly browned. Sprinkle lightly with powdered sugar. Let cool for 30 minutes before cutting.

Peach Squares

OVEN TEMPERATURE: 350 degrees

YIELD: 20 squares

½ cups flour
½ cup almonds, ground
⅓ cup sugar
1 teaspoon baking powder
½ teaspoon salt
¾ cup butter

2 egg yolks
1 (8 ounce) package cream cheese
⅓ cup sugar
2 egg whites
½ teaspoon almond extract
14 small peaches, pitted and sliced

In large bowl, stir together flour, almonds, sugar, baking powder, and salt. Cut butter into flour mixture with pastry blender. Beat egg yolks and add to dry mixture. Toss mixture with fork until all dry ingredients are moistened. Press dough into 13 x 9 x 2–inch baking ban. Bake for 20 minutes. In medium bowl, cream the cream cheese with sugar until fluffy. Beat in egg whites and almond extract just until combined. Spread over partially baked crust. Arrange peach slices on top of cream cheese until covered. Bake for 30 minutes. Cool for 30 minutes before cutting.

Chocolate Mint Squares

OVEN TEMPERATURE: 350 degrees   **YIELD:** 6½ dozen squares

2 (1 ounce) squares unsweetened
  chocolate
½ cup (1 stick) butter
2 eggs
1 cup sugar
½ cup flour
½ cup walnuts or pecans, chopped
1½ cups powdered sugar

3 tablespoons butter, softened
2 tablespoons whipping cream
¾ teaspoon mint or peppermint
  extract
1 to 2 drops green food coloring
2 (1 ounce) squares milk chocolate
2 tablespoons butter
1 teaspoon vanilla extract

In small saucepan, melt unsweetened chocolate and butter over *low* heat. Cool. In large bowl, beat eggs. Add sugar and beat until fluffy. Stir in flour, walnuts, and melted chocolate. Spoon mixture into greased 9-inch-square baking pan, spreading evenly. Bake for 25 minutes. Cool. Combine powdered sugar, butter, whipping cream, extract, and food coloring. Beat until smooth. Spread evenly over baked layer. Cover and refrigerate for 1 hour. Melt milk chocolate and butter. Stir in vanilla. Drizzle over mint layer. Cover and refrigerate for 1 hour. Cut into 1-inch squares.

S'mores Bars

OVEN TEMPERATURE: Broil

YIELD: 2 dozen bars

1½ cups graham cracker crumbs
  (about 20 squares)
5 tablespoons butter, melted
3 tablespoons sugar
2 tablespoons cocoa powder
¾ cups sugar
5 tablespoons flour

¼ teaspoon salt
1½ cups milk
½ teaspoon vanilla extract
2 egg yolks, beaten slightly
1 tablespoon butter
1 (10.5 ounce) bag mini
  marshmallows

Combine graham cracker crumbs, butter, and 3 tablespoons sugar. Stir until all crumbs are moistened. Use fork to achieve crumbly texture. Press into ungreased 11 x 9 x 2–inch baking pan. Bake for 8 minutes. Set aside. In saucepan, mix together cocoa, sugar, flour, salt, and milk. Bring to boil, stirring constantly until pudding is smooth and thick (about 5 minutes). Pour over crust. Let cool for 10 minutes. Add marshmallows to top. Put under broiler until marshmallows begin to turn brown. Cool for 10 minutes longer. Store in refrigerator for 2 hours before cutting into bars.

Baklava

OVEN TEMPERATURE: 350 degrees

YIELD: 3½ dozen squares

Ingredients for pastry:
1 pound frozen phyllo pastry
1 cup (2 sticks) butter, melted
1 cup walnuts, ground
1 cup almonds, ground
2 tablespoons sugar
½ teaspoon cinnamon
½ teaspoon nutmeg

Ingredients for syrup:
½ cup sugar
¼ cup water
1 tablespoon lemon juice
2½ tablespoons honey

After thawing, cut phyllo in half crosswise. Then cut each half to fit a 13 x 9 x 2–inch baking pan. Cover with damp towel. Lightly butter bottom of pan. Layer 10 sheets of phyllo in pan and brush each sheet with melted butter. Combine walnuts, almonds, sugar, and spices. Mix well. Sprinkle half of nut mixture over phyllo in pan. Drizzle with melted butter. Top nut mixture with 20 additional sheets of phyllo, brushing each with butter. Top with remaining nut mixture. Drizzle with melted butter. Top with remaining phyllo, brushing each sheet with melted butter. Using sharp knife, cut into diamond or square shapes all the way to bottom of pan. You may cut into 4 long rows then make diagonal cuts. Bake for 50 minutes or until baklava is golden and crisp. Cool thoroughly. For syrup, combine sugar, water, and lemon juice in small saucepan. Boil for 7 minutes. Add honey and boil 3 minutes longer. Drizzle over pastries.

Shortbread Bars

OVEN TEMPERATURE: 350 degrees

YIELD: 24 bars

Ingredients for crust:
1¼ cups flour
3 tablespoons light brown sugar
¼ teaspoon baking powder
½ cup (1 stick) butter

Ingredients for sauce:
¼ cup (½ stick) butter
⅓ cup sugar
⅓ cup light brown sugar, firmly packed
⅓ cup light corn syrup
1 tablespoon water
¼ teaspoon salt
½ cup walnuts, coarsely chopped
½ cup hazelnuts, coarsely chopped
¾ cup whipping cream
1 teaspoon vanilla extract

In medium bowl, combine flour, sugar, and baking powder for crust. Cut in butter with pastry blender until crumbly. Press into bottom of foil-lined 9 x 9 x 2–inch baking pan. Butter foil as well. Bake for 25 minutes. In medium sauce-pan, melt butter for filling. Stir in sugars, corn syrup, water, and salt. Stir in chopped nuts. Bring to boil over *medium-high* heat. Boil for 2 minutes, stirring often. Remove from heat and fold in cream and vanilla. Spread filling evenly over crust. Bake for 12 to 15 minutes. Cool thoroughly before cutting.

Chocolate Nut Bars

OVEN TEMPERATURE: 350 degrees

YIELD: 2½ dozen

2 cups flour
¾ cup (1½ sticks) butter, softened
1⅓ cup sugar
¾ teaspoon baking powder
¾ teaspoon cinnamon
1½ cups pecans, chopped
1 (6 ounce) package chocolate chips

¼ cup (½ stick) butter
1¼ cups light brown sugar, firmly packed
3 eggs
1 teaspoon vanilla extract
4 tablespoons powdered sugar, sifted

Combine flour, butter, sugar, baking powder, and cinnamon in large bowl. Beat together until blended and then work with fork until crumbly. Stir in nuts. Press into bottom of ungreased 13 x 9 x 2–inch baking pan. Bake for 15 to 18 minutes. While crust is still hot, melt chocolate chips and butter in saucepan over *low* heat. Stir constantly until smooth. Remove from heat. Stir in sugar, eggs, and vanilla. Pour over crust. Bake for 22 minutes or until center is set. Cool completely before sprinkling with powdered sugar and cutting into bars.

Reindeer Hoofprint Bars

OVEN TEMPERATURE: 300 degrees

YIELD: 25 bars

½ cup (1 stick) plus 2 tablespoons
   butter, softened
½ cup plus 2 tablespoons sugar
½ egg

1 teaspoon vanilla extract
1¼ cups flour
¼ teaspoon baking powder
⅛ teaspoon salt

In large bowl, cream together butter with sugar. Add half egg, and beat until fluffy. Stir in vanilla. In separate bowl, sift together flour, baking powder, and salt. Add to creamed mixture and stir until dry ingredients are incorporated. Turn batter into 13 x 9 x 2–inch baking pan and spread until smooth. Draw fork over dough with straight lines and curves to look like hoofprints. Bake for 30 minutes to a pale golden color. Remove from oven and cut into 5 strips each way. Cool completely before removing from pan.

Date Oats Squares

OVEN TEMPERATURE: 375 degrees

YIELD: 36 squares

1 (7¼ ounce) package pitted dates, chopped
⅔ cup boiling water
1 teaspoon lemon extract
½ cup walnuts, chopped
⅔ cup flour

½ teaspoon baking soda
½ teaspoon cinnamon
¼ teaspoon salt
⅔ cup light brown sugar, firmly packed
1½ cups quick oats
5 tablespoons butter, melted

In saucepan, combine dates and water. Stir over *medium* heat until it forms a medium-thick paste. Remove from heat and stir in extract and nuts. Cool. In large bowl, sift together flour, baking soda, cinnamon, and salt. With fork, stir in brown sugar and oats until blended. Drizzle melted butter over mixture and toss until well mixed. Spread half the mixture in 8 x 8 x 2–inch baking pan. Spread date mixture evenly over top of first layer. Crumble remaining oat mixture over dates and pat down gently. Bake for 20 to 22 minutes. Cool in pan. Cut into 6 strips each way.

Peanut Candy Squares

OVEN TEMPERATURE: 375 degrees

YIELD: 18 squares

2 tablespoons shortening
¼ cup peanut butter
1¼ cups light brown sugar, firmly
    packed
1 teaspoon vanilla extract

2 eggs
¾ cup flour
1 teaspoon baking powder
¼ teaspoon salt
½ cup roasted peanuts, chopped

In large bowl, cream shortening and peanut butter with brown sugar. Add vanilla and eggs and beat well. In separate bowl, sift together flour, baking powder, and salt. Add to creamed mixture in portions. Stir until all dry ingredients are well incorporated. Add peanuts. Stir until well distributed. Turn into greased 9 x 9 x 2–inch baking pan. Bake for 25 minutes. Cool completely before cutting into squares.

Holiday Fruit Bars

OVEN TEMPERATURE: 350 degrees

YIELD: 30 bars

¼ pound moist candied citron, sliced thin and cut fine
¾ cup dates, pitted and cut fine
½ cup golden raisins
½ cup moist figs, chopped
1 cup pecans or walnuts, chopped
½ cup light molasses or honey
1 teaspoon brandy extract
5 tablespoons butter, softened

½ cup sugar
2 eggs
½ cups flour
½ teaspoon baking powder
½ teaspoon cinnamon
¼ teaspoon nutmeg
¼ teaspoon salt
2 tablespoons buttermilk

Combine fruit and nuts in bowl. Add molasses or honey and extract and stir enough to blend. Let set for at least 30 minutes. In large bowl, cream butter with sugar. Beat in eggs, one at a time, stirring after each until fluffy. In separate bowl, sift flour, baking powder, spices, and salt. Add flour mixture and buttermilk to creamed mixture in alternating portions until all dry ingredients are incorporated. Stir in fruit and nut mixture until well distributed. Spread batter in 13 x 9 x 2–inch baking pan. Bake for 20 minutes. Remove to cake rack and mark top immediately into 6 strips one way and 5 strips the other way. Cut into bars. Finish cooling before removing from pan. Place waxed paper between bars when storing.

German Chocolate Brownies

OVEN TEMPERATURE: 350 degrees

YIELD: 16 squares

1 (1 ounce) square semisweet
   chocolate
¾ cup sugar
½ cup (1 stick) butter
2 eggs
1 tablespoon canola oil
1 teaspoon vanilla extract
1¼ cups flour
3 tablespoons cocoa powder

1 teaspoon baking powder
½ teaspoon salt
⅔ cup (1 stick plus 2 tablespoons)
   butter
⅓ cup light brown sugar, firmly packed
⅓ cup light corn syrup
1 cup flaked coconut
¾ cup pecans, copped
1 teaspoon vanilla extract

In saucepan, combine chocolate, sugar, and butter over *low* heat. Sir constantly until melted. Remove from heat to cool. In large bowl, beat eggs, oil, and vanilla. Stir in chocolate mixture until well blended. In separate bowl, sift together flour, cocoa powder, baking powder, and salt. Add to chocolate mixture in portions. Stir until all dry ingredients are well incorporated. Turn into greased 8 x 8 x 2–inch baking pan. Bake for 35 minutes. Cool completely. In saucepan, melt butter over *medium* heat. Add brown sugar and corn syrup. Stir constantly until thick. Remove from heat. Add coconut, pecans, and vanilla. Stir well. Spread over brownies. Let set for 5 minutes before cutting into bars.

Brazil Nut Orange Bars

OVEN TEMPERATURE: 375 degrees   **YIELD:** 3 dozen

1 cup flour
¼ teaspoon salt
¼ cup (½ stick) butter, cut into pieces
2 eggs, well beaten
¾ cup light brown sugar, firmly packed
1 cup Brazil nuts, finely chopped

1 tablespoon orange peel, finely grated
1 tablespoon orange juice
½ cup flaked coconut
1 teaspoon vanilla extract
¼ teaspoon salt
2 tablespoons flour

In medium bowl, sift together flour and salt. Cut in butter with pastry blender. Use fork to mix until crumbly. Press into 9 x 9 x 2–inch baking pan. Bake for 15 minutes. In same bowl, mix together eggs and brown sugar. Blend well. Add nuts, orange peel, orange juice, coconut, vanilla, salt, and flour. Mix well. Spread evenly over baked crust. Bake 15 minutes. Cool in pan before cutting into bars.

Pistachio Chocolate Chews

OVEN TEMPERATURE: 350 degrees

YIELD: 24 squares

½ cup (1 stick) butter
2 (1 ounce) squares unsweetened
  chocolate
2 eggs, slightly beaten

1 cup sugar
½ teaspoon vanilla extract
½ cup plus 1 tablespoon sifted flour
¾ cup pistachio nuts, chopped

In saucepan, melt butter and chocolate. Cool slightly. In medium bowl, mix together eggs, sugar, and vanilla. Add chocolate mixture. Stir well. Add flour. Mix well. Turn into 11 x 7 x 2–inch baking pan. Bake 35 to 40 minutes. Cool in pan before cutting into squares.

Peppermint Cream Brownies

OVEN TEMPERATURE: 350 degrees

YIELD: 18 bars

Ingredients for brownies:
2 (1 ounce) squares unsweetened
  chocolate
5 tablespoons butter
½ teaspoon vanilla extract
¾ cup sugar
2 eggs
⅔ cup flour
¼ teaspoon baking powder
⅛ teaspoon salt
1 tablespoon milk
½ cup walnuts, chopped

Ingredients for peppermint butter cream:
2 tablespoons butter, softened
1 cup powdered sugar, sifted and
  firmly packed
1 tablespoon hot milk
Drop red food coloring
⅛ teaspoon peppermint extract or 2
  drops oil of peppermint
2 teaspoons light corn syrup
⅛ teaspoon salt

In saucepan, melt chocolate over low heat. Cool. In large bowl, cream butter and vanilla until smooth; add sugar gradually, creaming well. Beat in eggs, one at a time, stirring until fluffy. Stir in chocolate. In separate bowl, sift together flour, baking powder, and salt. Add flour mixture to creamed mixture in portions, adding milk after first portion. Stir until all dry ingredients are well incorporated. Add walnuts just until distributed in batter. Divide dough in half and spread half in each of two waxed paper–lined 8 x 8 x 2–inch baking pans. Bake for 20 minutes. Cool on rack. Loosen waxed paper from bottom of layers and invert 1 layer on cake plate. For peppermint butter cream, cream butter with sugar and add hot milk gradually. Add enough food coloring to give it a delicate pink. Stir in enough flavoring to taste, corn syrup, and salt. Beat until smooth, spreading consistency. When layers are barely cool, spread with peppermint cream. Place second layer on top, right side up, and press two layers together. Cut into 6 strips one way and 3 strips the other.

Dulce de Leche Bars

OVEN TEMPERATURE: 350 degrees   **YIELD:** 2 dozen

¼ cup (½ stick) butter
1 (10.5 ounce) bag mini
marshmallows

6 cups toasted oats cereal
1 cup golden raisins
1 (11 ounce) bag butterscotch chips

In saucepan, melt butter and marshmallows over *medium* heat. In large bowl, combine cereal, raisins, and butterscotch chips. Pour melted mixture over cereal mixture and stir until all ingredients are well incorporated. Press into 13 x 9 x 2–inch baking pan. Cool in pan for 1 hour before cutting into squares.

Pineapple Nut Brownies

OVEN TEMPERATURE: 350 degrees

YIELD: 16 squares

- 2 (1 ounce) squares unsweetened chocolate
- ½ cup shortening
- 1 cup sugar
- 2 eggs, well beaten
- 1 (9 ounce) can crushed pineapple, drained
- ½ teaspoon vanilla extract
- 1 cup flour
- ½ teaspoon baking powder
- ¼ teaspoon baking soda
- ¼ teaspoon salt
- ½ cup nuts, chopped

In heavy saucepan, melt chocolate with shortening. Blend in sugar. Remove from heat. Add eggs, pineapple, and vanilla. Beat well. In separate bowl, sift together flour, baking powder, baking soda, and salt. Add to creamed mixture and blend well. Add nuts. Stir until well distributed. Turn into greased 8 x 8 x 2-inch baking pan. Bake for 35 to 40 minutes. Cool in pan. Cut into squares.

Walnut Sticks

OVEN TEMPERATURE: 350 degrees   **YIELD:** 24 sticks

Ingredients for part 1:
½ cup (1 stick) butter, softened
½ cup light brown sugar, firmly packed
1¼ cups flour

Ingredients for part 2:
2 tablespoons flour
¾ cup light brown sugar, firmly packed
½ teaspoon baking powder
1 egg, beaten
½ teaspoon vanilla extract
¼ teaspoon almond extract
¼ cup flaked coconut, firmly packed
½ cup walnuts, chopped
⅓ cup powdered sugar, sifted

In large bowl, cream together butter and sugar. Add flour in portions, working until all flour is incorporated and smooth, stiff dough is formed. Place dough into 13 x 9 x 2–inch baking pan. Press into thin, even layer. Bake for 13 minutes. Cool on cake rack. In separate bowl, combine flour, brown sugar, and baking powder. Add egg and both extracts. Stir well. Stir in coconut and walnuts. Spread mixture evenly over cooled baked layer. Return to oven and bake 15 to 18 minutes, until top looks slightly underbaked. Cool slightly in pan. Sift powdered sugar over top, before cutting into 6 strips lengthwise and 4 crosswise.

Pecan Pie Bars

OVEN TEMPERATURE: 350 degrees   **YIELD:** 3 dozen bars

1½ cups flour
½ cup (1 stick) butter, softened
¼ cup light brown sugar, firmly packed
2 tablespoons butter, melted
¾ cup sugar

3 eggs
¾ cup light corn syrup
1 teaspoon vanilla extract
1 (12 ounce) package chocolate chips
1½ cups pecans, coarsely chopped

Work flour, butter, and brown sugar together until crumbly. Press into greased 13 x 9 x 2–inch baking pan. Bake for 12 to 15 minutes or until lightly browned. For filling, cream 2 tablespoons butter with sugar in large bowl. Add eggs, one at a time, stirring after each. Add corn syrup and vanilla and stir well. Add chocolate chips and pecans. Stir until well distributed in batter. Pour over hot crust. Bake for 30 minutes or until center is set. Cool completely in pan before cutting.

Pumpkin Harvest Bars

OVEN TEMPERATURE: 350 degrees

YIELD: 16

¾ cup sugar
½ cup applesauce
½ cup canned pumpkin
1 whole egg
1 egg white
2 tablespoons canola oil
1¾ cups flour
2 teaspoons baking powder

½ teaspoon salt
1 teaspoon cinnamon
½ teaspoon nutmeg
¼ teaspoon ginger
¼ teaspoon cloves
1 teaspoon grated orange peel
½ cup raisins

In large bowl, combine sugar, applesauce, pumpkin, whole egg, egg white, and oil. In separate bowl, sift together flour, baking powder, salt, and spices. Add flour mixture to applesauce mixture. Stir until all dry ingredients are well incorporated. Add orange peel and raisins. Stir well. Spread batter into greased 13 x 9 x 2–inch baking pan. Bake 25 to 30 minutes. Cool completely before cutting into squares.

Chocolate-Covered Strawberries Bars

OVEN TEMPERATURE: 350 degrees

YIELD: 3 dozen bars

1 cup (2 sticks) butter, softened
½ cup light brown sugar, firmly packed
2 cups flour
¼ teaspoon salt
1 (12 ounce package) semisweet chocolate chips, divided

1 (14 ounce) can sweetened condensed milk
½ cup nuts, chopped
⅓ cup seedless strawberry whole fruit preserves

In large bowl, cream butter with sugar. Add flour and salt. Stir well with fork until crumbly. Press 1¾ cups of crumb mixture into 13 x 9 x 2–inch baking pan. Keep remainder for later. Bake for 10 to 12 minutes. In saucepan, combine 1 cup of chocolate chips and sweetened condensed milk over medium heat. Stir until chips are melted and mixture is smooth. Spread over hot crust. Add nuts to reserved crumb mixture. Sprinkle over chocolate layer. Drop spoonfuls of fruit preserves over crumb mixture. Sprinkle remaining chocolate chips over top. Bake for 25 to 30 minutes. Cool completely before cutting into bars.

Peanut Butter Molasses Squares

OVEN TEMPERATURE: 375 degrees

YIELD: 2 dozen squares

⅓ cup shortening
½ cup peanut butter
½ cup sugar
1 egg
½ cup light molasses
1½ cups flour

1½ teaspoons baking powder
¼ teaspoon baking soda
½ teaspoon salt
½ cup hot water
½ cup peanuts, finely chopped

In large bowl, cream shortening and peanut butter with sugar until fluffy. Add egg and molasses and beat well. In separate bowl, sift together flour, baking powder, baking soda, and salt. Add to creamed mixture alternately with hot water. Stir until all dry ingredients are well incorporated. Turn into greased 13 x 9 x 2–inch baking pan. Bake for 30 to 35 minutes. Cool completely before cutting into squares.

Peanut Butter Marshmallow Bars

REFRIGERATE: 2 hours

YIELD: 3 dozen

5 tablespoons butter
½ cup creamy peanut butter
1 (16 ounce) bag marshmallows

¼ teaspoon salt
4½ cups pre-sweetened puffed wheat
    cereal, slightly crushed

In saucepan, melt butter, peanut butter, and marshmallows over *low* heat, stirring constantly. Add salt. Put cereal in large bowl and pour peanut butter mixture over top. Stir until cereal is well coated. Press into buttered 9 x 9 x 2–inch baking pan. Refrigerate. Cut into squares.

No-Bake Cookies

Like snowflakes, my Christmas memories gather and dance—each beautiful, unique, and too soon gone.

DEBORAH WHIPP

Coconut Date Cookies

REFRIGERATE: 2 hours

YIELD: 2 dozen

¾ cup sugar
1 cup dates, pitted and chopped
2 eggs, well beaten
1 teaspoon vanilla extract

1 cup walnuts, chopped
1 cup cornflakes cereal
1 cup sugar-coated toasted rice cereal
1⅓ cups flaked coconut

In heavy skillet combine sugar, dates, and eggs. Cook over *medium* heat until mixture begins to thicken (about 5 minutes). Remove from heat and stir in vanilla and walnuts. Carefully stir in cereal. Cool slightly. Dip hands in cold water and then shape mixture into small mounds. Roll in coconut and place on cookie sheets. Refrigerate.

Holiday Bonbons

LET STAND: Until set

YIELD: 6 dozen

1 (14 ounce) can sweetened
    condensed milk
½ cup (1 stick) butter, softened
2 cups powdered sugar

1 (12 ounce) package grated coconut
2 (12 ounce) bag semisweet chocolate
    chips
4 tablespoons vegetable shortening

Mix together milk, butter, sugar, and coconut. Cover with waxed paper and chill. In saucepan, melt chocolate chips and shortening. Roll coconut mixture into balls and dip each into chocolate mixture. Drop onto waxed paper to cool.

Christmas Snowballs

REFRIGERATE: Until firm

YIELD: 5 dozen

2 cups white chocolate chips
¼ cup plus 2 tablespoons heavy cream

1 cup finely ground almonds
1½ cups sweetened flaked coconut

Place chocolate chips and ¼ cup of cream in saucepan. Stir constantly until melted and smooth. Sir in additional cream and almonds. Spread mixture in lightly greased 8 x 8–inch baking pan. Chill until firm. Cut into 1-inch squares and roll into balls. Then roll balls in coconut.

Holiday Hustle Chocolate Cookies

LET STAND: Until set

YIELD: 5 dozen

½ cup (1 stick) butter
¼ cup cocoa powder
2 cups sugar
½ cup milk

½ cup peanut butter
3 cups oats
1 cup nuts, chopped

Bring butter, cocoa, sugar, and milk to a boil over *medium* heat. Stir constantly. Remove from heat and add peanut butter, oats, and nuts. Mix well. Drop by spoonfuls onto waxed paper until cool. When they are no longer sticky, store in airtight container.

Haystacks

LET STAND: Until firm

YIELD: 3 dozen

2 cups sugar
½ cup (1 stick) butter
½ cup milk
4 tablespoons cocoa powder

3 cups quick oats
½ cup peanut butter
½ cup flaked coconut

In saucepan, combine sugar, butter, milk, and cocoa. Bring to hard boil. Remove from burner and add oats, peanut butter, and coconut. Stir until well blended. Drop by spoonfuls onto waxed paper. Let sit until firm.

Chinese Christmas Cookies

REFRIGERATE: 2 hours

YIELD: 2 dozen

1 cup semisweet chocolate chips
1 cup peanut butter chips

1 cup chow mein noodles
1 cup roasted peanuts

In heavy saucepan, melt chocolate and peanut butter chips, stirring continually until smooth. Combine chow mein noodles and peanuts in large mixing bowl. Pour chocolate mixture over noodles and nuts and stir until coated. Drop by spoonfuls onto parchment paper–lined cookie sheet. Refrigerate.

Danish Christmas Cookies

REFRIGERATE: Do not refrigerate   **YIELD:** 2 dozen

¼ cup (½ stick) butter
⅔ cup sugar
1 egg, beaten
1 cup dates, pitted and finely chopped

1 teaspoon vanilla extract
2 cups crispy rice cereal
¾ cup walnuts, finely chopped
1 cup sweetened flaked coconut

In saucepan, combine butter, sugar, egg, and dates. Cook over *medium* heat until thickened (8 to 10 minutes). Remove from heat. Stir in vanilla. In large bowl, combine rice cereal and walnuts. Stir in date mixture and blend well. Taking one spoonful of mixture at a time, form into 1-inch balls. Roll balls in coconut. Place on parchment paper until set.

Hazelnut Crispy Treats

REFRIGERATE: 30 minutes

YIELD: 16 to 20 bars

3 cups crispy rice cereal
½ cup dates, chopped
½ cup hazelnuts, chopped
½ cup light brown sugar, firmly packed

½ cup light corn syrup
1 tablespoon butter
½ cup chocolate-hazelnut spread

In large bowl, combine cereal, dates, and nuts. In small saucepan, combine brown sugar, corn syrup, and butter. Just barely bring to boil, stirring constantly. Remove from heat and add chocolate-hazelnut spread. Pour sugar mixture over cereal mixture and stir until coated. Line 8 x 8 x 2–inch baking pan with foil and grease foil. Press mixture into bottom of pan. Refrigerate for 30 minutes or let stand for 2 hours before cutting bars.

Chocolate Nutties

REFRIGERATE: 2 hours

YIELD: 2 dozen

2 (12 ounce) bags semisweet chocolate chips
1 (12 ounce) bag butterscotch chips
2 cups crunchy peanut butter

1 cup pecans or walnuts, coarsely chopped
1 (16 ounce) bag mini marshmallows

In heavy saucepan, melt chocolate and butterscotch chips over *low* heat. Stir in peanut butter and nuts. Remove from heat and cool slightly. Add marshmallows and stir until well coated. Pour into greased 13 x 9 x 2-inch baking pan. Refrigerate.

Chewy Chocolate No-Bakes

REFRIGERATE: 2 to 3 hours

YIELD: 3 dozen

1 cup semisweet chocolate chips
16 large marshmallows
5 tablespoons butter

2 cups oats
1 cup dried mixed fruit, diced
1 teaspoon vanilla extract

In large saucepan over *low* heat, melt chocolate chips, marshmallows, and butter, stirring until smooth. Remove from heat; cool slightly. Stir in oats, mixed fruit, and vanilla. Drop by rounded spoonfuls onto waxed paper. Chill 2 to 3 hours. Let stand at room temperature about 15 minutes before serving.

No-Bake Gingersnap Balls

REFRIGERATE: 1 hour

YIELD: 2 dozen

20 gingersnap cookies (about 5 ounces)
3 tablespoons dark corn syrup

2 tablespoons creamy peanut butter
⅓ cup powdered sugar

Place cookies in large resealable plastic food storage bag. Crush with rolling pin. Combine corn syrup and peanut butter in medium bowl. Add crushed gingersnaps. Mix well. (Mixture should hold together without being sticky. If mixture is too dry, stir in additional 1 to 2 tablespoons of corn syrup.) Shape mixture into 1-inch balls. Roll in powdered sugar. Refrigerate.

Banana Peanut Butter Fudge Bars

REFRIGERATE: 2 hours

YIELD: 2 dozen

⅔ cup (1 stick plus 2 tablespoons) butter
2 teaspoons vanilla extract
2½ cups oats
½ cup light brown sugar, firmly packed

1¼ cups (about 1 large) overripe banana, finely chopped
1 cup semisweet chocolate chips
½ cup peanut butter

Melt butter in large skillet over *medium* heat; stir in vanilla. Add oats and brown sugar. Heat and stir constantly for 5 minutes. Set aside ¾ cup oat mixture. Press remaining oat mixture into greased 9 x 9 x 2–inch square baking pan. Sprinkle banana over crust. Melt chocolate chips and peanut butter together over *low* heat. Pour over banana mixture and spread evenly. Sprinkle with reserved oat mixture. Press down lightly.

Gift of the Magi No-Bake Squares

REFRIGERATE: Until firm

YIELD: 3 dozen squares

Ingredients for crust:
½ cup (1 stick) butter
¼ cup sugar
¼ cup cocoa powder
1 egg
¼ teaspoon salt
1½ cups graham cracker crumbs
¾ cup flaked coconut
½ cup pecans, chopped

Ingredients for filling:
⅓ cup butter, softened
½ (8 ounce) package cream cheese, softened
1 teaspoon vanilla extract
1 cup powdered sugar

Ingredients for glaze:
1 (2 ounce) dark or bittersweet chocolate candy bar, broken into half-inch pieces
1 teaspoon butter

In saucepan, combine butter, sugar, cocoa powder, egg, and salt. Cook over *medium* heat, stirring constantly. Add cracker crumbs, coconut, and pecans. Press into 9 x 9 x 2–inch square baking pan that has been lined with foil, shiny side up. Allow 2 inches of foil to overhang sides. In small bowl, beat together butter, cream cheese, and vanilla until smooth. Gradually beat in powdered sugar. Spread over crust. Refrigerate for 30 minutes. For glaze, place candy bar pieces and butter in sealed plastic baggie. Microwave on *high* for 50 seconds. Turn bag over and microwave for another 45 seconds. Knead bag until chocolate is smooth. Cut off corner of bag and drizzle chocolate over filling. Refrigerate. Use foil to remove bars from pan. Cut into squares.

Sunrise Cherry Crisps

LET STAND: 1 hour

YIELD: 3 dozen

¼ cup (½ stick) butter, softened
1 cup peanut butter
1 cup powdered sugar
1⅓ cups crisp rice cereal
½ cup maraschino cherries, drained, dried, and chopped

¼ cup plus 2 tablespoons mini semisweet chocolate chips
¼ cup pecans, chopped
1 to 2 cups flaked coconut

In large bowl, cream butter and peanut butter with sugar. Stir in cereal, cherries, chocolate chips, and pecans. Mix well. Take spoonfuls of dough and create 1-inch balls. Roll in coconut. Place on cookie sheets and chill.

Marshmallow Delights

REFRIGERATE: Until firm

YIELD: 5 dozen

2 cups sugar
3 tablespoons cocoa powder
1 cup evaporated milk
6 tablespoons butter

1 (8 ounce) bag mini marshmallows
3⅔ cups graham cracker crumbs
(about 30 whole graham crackers)

Combine sugar, cocoa powder, and milk in large saucepan over *medium* heat. Bring to boil and continue to boil for 5 minutes, stirring constantly. Remove from heat and stir in butter and marshmallows. Stir until marshmallows are melted and mixture is smooth and creamy. Stir in graham cracker crumbs. Drop by spoonfuls onto waxed paper.

Crispy Date Cookies

REFRIGERATE: 2 hours

YIELD: 2½ dozen

½ cup (1 stick) butter
1 cup sugar
1 cup dates, chopped
1 egg, beaten

1 teaspoon vanilla extract
2¼ cups crispy rice cereal
1 cup powdered sugar

In large saucepan, melt butter over *low* heat. Remove from heat and add sugar and dates. Mix well. Return to heat and cook, stirring constantly, for 4 to 5 minutes. To achieve best result, keep heat *low* and stir vigorously. Add egg, and cook, stirring constantly, until all ingredients are well blended. Return to heat and cook, stirring constantly, for 4 minutes. Add vanilla and cereal. Remove from heat and stir until all dry ingredients are well incorporated. Take dough in spoonfuls and roll into balls. Roll in powdered sugar and cool for 20 minutes. Store in refrigerator.

Peanut Butter Fudgies

REFRIGERATE: 2 hours

YIELD: 2 dozen

2 cups sugar
½ cup milk
½ cup cocoa powder
⅛ teaspoon salt

½ cup (1 stick) butter
1 cup peanut butter
1 teaspoon vanilla extract
3 cups quick-cooking oats

In large saucepan, combine sugar, milk, cocoa, salt, and butter and mix well. Bring to boil and continue boiling for 1 minute without stirring. It's important to boil until all sugar crystals are dissolved. Remove from heat and stir in peanut butter and vanilla until smooth. Add oats and mix well. (Do not use regular or instant oats.) Let mixture stand for 10 minutes, stirring occasionally. Drop by spoonfuls onto waxed paper–lined baking sheets. Cool until no longer sticky. Shape into balls. Cool completely. Store at room temperature.

Pineapple Marmalade Squares

REFRIGERATE: 2 hours

YIELD: 16 servings

1 cup graham cracker crumbs
2 tablespoons sugar
¼ cup (½ stick) butter, melted
1 cup sour cream
4 ounces cream cheese, softened

½ cup sugar
¼ cup orange marmalade or apricot
  spread, divided
1 (20 ounce) can crushed pineapple
1 envelope unflavored gelatin

Combine cracker crumbs, 2 tablespoons sugar, and butter in small bowl. Press mixture into 8 x 8 x 2–inch baking pan. Freeze for 10 minutes. In medium bowl, cream sour cream and cream cheese with sugar. Add 1 tablespoon of marmalade. Stir until smooth. Drain crushed pineapple, reserving ¼ cup of juice. In small saucepan, sprinkle gelatin over reserved juice. Let stand 1 minute. Cool and stir over *low* heat until dissolved. Beat gelatin mixture into sour cream mixture. Spoon over crust. Stir together crushed pineapple and remaining marmalade. Spoon evenly over sour cream filling. Cover and refrigerate.

Holiday Caramel Squares

REFRIGERATE: 2 hours

YIELD: 18 squares

1 cup light brown sugar, firmly packed
1 egg, beaten
⅓ cup butter
⅓ cup milk
1 cup flaked coconut
1 cup nuts, chopped
¾ cup graham cracker crumbs

1 teaspoon vanilla extract
18 to 20 whole graham crackers
1¼ cups powdered sugar
¼ teaspoon vanilla extract
2 tablespoons milk
½ cup graham cracker crumbs

In saucepan, combine sugar, egg, butter, and milk. Bring to rolling boil. Remove from heat. Cool. Add coconut, nuts, cracker crumbs, and vanilla. Mix well. Line bottom of 13 x 9 x 2–inch baking pan with whole graham crackers. Spread coconut mixture over crackers. Add second layer of graham crackers. In small bowl, combine powdered sugar, vanilla, and milk. Mix well. Spread over graham crackers. Sprinkle with graham cracker crumbs. Refrigerate. Cut into squares.

Chocolate Peanut Butter Bars

REFRIGERATE: 1 hour

YIELD: 18 squares

1¼ cups peanut butter
¾ cup (1½ sticks) butter, softened
2 cups powdered sugar
3 cups graham cracker crumbs

2 cups semisweet chocolate chips, divided
¾ cup peanut butter

In large bowl, cream peanut butter and butter with 1 cup of powdered sugar. With wooden spoon work in remaining powdered sugar, cracker crumbs, and ½ cup of chocolate chips. Press mixture evenly into 13 x 9 x 2–inch baking pan. Smooth top with spatula. Melt peanut butter and remaining chocolate chips in saucepan over *low* heat. Stir constantly until smooth. Spread over graham cracker crust. Refrigerate. Cut into bars. Store in refrigerator.

Citrus Cream Bars

REFRIGERATE: 2 hours

YIELD: 2 dozen bars

1¼ cups chocolate sandwich cookies, finely crushed
⅔ cup (1 stick plus 2 tablespoons) butter, softened, divided
1½ cups powdered sugar

1½ teaspoons grated orange peel
½ teaspoon grated lemon peel
½ teaspoon vanilla extract
¼ cup semisweet chocolate chips, melted

In medium bowl, combine cookie crumbs and half of butter. Press into ungreased 9 x 9 x 2–inch square baking pan. Refrigerate until firm. In small bowl, combine powdered sugar, remaining butter, milk, orange peel, lemon peel, and vanilla. Beat on *medium* speed with electric mixer, scraping bowl often. Beat until mixture is light and fluffy. Spread over crust. Drizzle melted chocolate over filling. Refrigerate. Cut into bars. Store in refrigerator.

Christmas Eve Snack Bars

REFRIGERATE: 1 hour

YIELD: 3 dozen

½ cup butter-flavored shortening
¾ cup peanut butter
2 cups powdered sugar, sifted
1 cup graham cracker crumbs

½ cup semisweet chocolate chips
½ cup graham cracker crumbs
½ cup crushed peanuts
¼ cup colored sugar crystals

In large bowl, cream shortening and peanut butter with powdered sugar. Stir in 1 cup cracker crumbs and chocolate chips. Cover and refrigerate. Take spoonfuls of dough and roll into 1-inch balls. Roll in ½ cup crumbs. Roll in peanuts. Roll in sugar crystals. Cover and store in refrigerator.

Honey Fudge Cookies

LET STAND: 2 hours

YIELD: 36 balls

2 cups sugar
½ cup cocoa powder
½ cup (1 stick) butter
⅛ teaspoon salt
½ cup milk

½ cup crunchy peanut butter
⅓ cup honey
1 teaspoon vanilla extract
3 cups oats

In saucepan, combine sugar, cocoa, butter, salt, and milk. Bring to boil and boil for 1 minute. Stir in peanut butter, honey, and vanilla. Blend well. Place oats in large bowl. Pour chocolate mixture over cereal. Stir until all cereal is well coated. Drop by spoonfuls onto waxed or parchment paper.

Chocolate Honey Crunchies

REFRIGERATE: 2 hours

YIELD: 2 dozen

2 cups milk chocolate chips
4 tablespoons milk
6 tablespoons honey

2 cups puffed rice cereal
⅓ cup peanuts, chopped
⅓ cup pecans, chopped

In saucepan, combine chocolate chips, milk, and honey. Stir constantly over *low* heat until chips are melted and mixture is smooth. Put cereal in large bowl. Add peanuts and pecans and stir well. Pour chocolate mixture over top. Stir until cereal mixture is well coated. Cover and refrigerate 2 hours. Remove from refrigerator and take dough in spoonfuls. Shape into 1-inch balls. Store in refrigerator.

Sweet Temptation Cookies

REFRIGERATE: Don't refrigerate

YIELD: 2 dozen

12 peanut-chocolate candies, crushed
¼ cup creamy or crunchy peanut
butter

¾ cup vanilla wafers, finely crushed
1 tablespoon cream or evaporated
milk

In saucepan, combine candies and peanut butter over *low* heat. Stir constantly until smooth. Blend in vanilla wafer crumbs and cream. Drop by spoonfuls onto waxed or parchment paper. Flatten slightly with back of buttered spoon. Store in refrigerator.

Reindeer Snacks

LET STAND: 1 hour   **YIELD:** 18 squares

1 cup quick oats
1½ cups crispy rice cereal
½ cup raisins
½ cup light brown sugar, firmly packed

½ cup light corn syrup
½ cup crunchy peanut butter
1 teaspoon vanilla extract

In large bowl, stir together oats, cereal, and raisins. Set aside. In saucepan, combine sugar and corn syrup over *medium* heat. Bring just to boiling and remove from heat. Stir in peanut butter and vanilla until smooth. Pour over dry mixture and mix well. Use piece of waxed paper to press mixture into greased 13 x 9 x 2–inch baking pan. Cool completely before cutting into squares.

Rolled and Shaped Cookies

Christmas may be a day of feasting or of prayer,
but always it will be a day of remembrance—a day in
which we think of everything we have ever loved.

AUGUSTA E. RUNDEL

Childhood Thumbprints

OVEN TEMPERATURE: 300 degrees   **YIELD:** 4 dozen

1 cup (2 sticks) butter, softened
⅔ cup sugar
2 egg yolks
½ teaspoons vanilla extract

2¼ cups flour
½ teaspoon salt
½ cup multicolored sugar crystals

In large bowl, cream butter with sugar, beating until light and fluffy. Add egg yolks one at a time, beating well after each. Stir in vanilla. Sift together flour and salt. Add flour mixture to creamed mixture. Chill for 1 hour. Roll into 1-inch balls and place about 2 inches apart on ungreased cookie sheets. Press thumb into each cookie. Bake for 20 to 25 minutes. Do not brown. Sprinkle with sugar crystals. Cool for 5 minutes before removing from pan.

Christmas Cream Cheesers

OVEN TEMPERATURE: 325 degrees

YIELD: 4 dozen

1 cup (2 sticks) butter, softened
1 (8 ounce) package cream cheese, softened
1 cup sugar
½ teaspoon vanilla extract

2½ cups flour
½ teaspoon salt
½ cup pecans, finely chopped
1 cup sugar crystals

In large bowl, cream butter, cream cheese, and sugar. Add vanilla and beat until fluffy. In separate bowl, sift together flour and salt. Gradually add flour mixture to creamed mixture until all dry ingredients are incorporated. Stir in pecans. Cover and refrigerate for 15 minutes. Shape dough into four 6-inch rolls about 1½ inches wide. Wrap in foil and refrigerate overnight. Remove one roll at a time and coat in sugar crystals. Cut slices ¼ inch thick. Place on foil-lined cookie sheets and bake for 15 to 18 minutes or until bottoms are light brown. Cool for 5 minutes before removing from pan.

German Christmas Cookies

OVEN TEMPERATURE: 375 degrees

YIELD: 2 dozen

1 cup honey
¾ cup light brown sugar, firmly packed
1 egg, beaten
1 tablespoon lemon juice
2¼ cups flour
½ teaspoon baking soda
½ teaspoon salt
¾ teaspoon cinnamon
½ teaspoon allspice
½ teaspoon nutmeg
¼ teaspoon cloves
¼ cup almonds, finely chopped
⅓ cup candied citron, finely chopped
12 candied red cherries, halved
48 whole almonds, blanched
1 cup plus 2 tablespoons powdered sugar, sifted
¼ cup plus 1 tablespoon water

In saucepan, heat honey until warm. Stir in brown sugar, egg, and lemon juice. Set aside. In large bowl, sift together flour, baking soda, salt, and spices. Add honey mixture, almonds, and citron. Stir until blended. Cover and refrigerate overnight. Divide dough into 4 parts and work with only one at a time, keeping remaining dough in refrigerator. On heavily floured surface, roll dough into ⅜-inch thickness. Cut dough with 2½-inch cookie or biscuit cutter. Place on greased cookie sheets. Press candied cherry half into center of each and arrange one almond on each side of the cherry, radiating outward. Bake for 12 minutes or until golden brown. Combine powdered sugar and water. Stir until blended. Brush cookies with mixture while still hot. Allow to cool for 5 minutes before transferring to wire rack to cool completely. Cookies will be hard and crunchy. To soften, store in an airtight container for 2 weeks.

Toasted Almond Fingers

OVEN TEMPERATURE: 325 degrees

YIELD: 4 dozen

1 cup (2 sticks) butter, softened
¾ cup powdered sugar, sifted
1 tablespoon milk
1 teaspoon vanilla extract
2 cups flour
¼ teaspoon salt

2 cups almonds, toasted and finely
  chopped
1 (6 ounce) package semisweet
  chocolate chips
1 tablespoon shortening

In large bowl, cream butter with sugar until fluffy. Beat in milk and vanilla. Sift together flour and salt. Add to creamed mixture in small portions until all dry ingredients are incorporated. Stir in almonds. Refrigerate dough for 1 hour. Take 1 tablespoon of dough and shape into a 2-inch finger. Place fingers on ungreased cookie sheets and bake for 15 to 17 minutes. Cool. Melt chocolate and shortening over *low* heat. Dip one end of each finger in chocolate, letting excess drip off. Cool on wire racks until set.

Cinnamon Snickerdoodles

OVEN TEMPERATURE: 375 degrees

YIELD: 5 dozen

⅓ cup sugar
1 tablespoon cinnamon
½ cup (1 stick) butter, softened
½ (8 ounce) package of cream cheese,
  softened

1 cup sugar
½ teaspoon baking powder
1 egg
1 teaspoon vanilla
2⅔ cup flour, sifted

In small bowl, combine ⅓ cup sugar and cinnamon. Set aside. In large bowl, cream butter and cream cheese with 1 cup sugar. Stir in baking powder. Beat in egg and vanilla. Incorporate flour in small portions. Divide dough in half. Between 2 sheets of waxed paper, roll one portion of dough at a time into a 12 x 8–inch rectangle. Remove top sheet of waxed paper and sprinkle with cinnamon-sugar mixture. Starting with short side, roll into log, removing waxed paper as you go. Roll each log in cinnamon/sugar mixture and wrap in plastic wrap. Refrigerate for 3 hours. Cut dough into slices ¼-inch thick and place on ungreased cookie sheets. Bake for 8 to 10 minutes. Cool for 5 minutes before removing from pan.

Spicy Molasses Cookies

OVEN TEMPERATURE: 375 degrees

YIELD: 4½ dozen

⅓ cup butter, softened
¼ cup dark brown sugar, firmly packed
⅓ cup molasses
1⅓ cups flour
½ teaspoon ginger

½ teaspoon apple pie spice
¼ teaspoon cloves
¼ teaspoon cardamom
⅛ teaspoon red pepper

In large bowl, cream butter with brown sugar and molasses. In separate bowl, sift together flour, spices, and red pepper. Add to creamed mixture and beat until well incorporated. Divide dough in half. Wrap and refrigerate for 1 hour. On floured surface, roll one part of dough at a time to $\frac{1}{16}$-inch thickness. Cut with 2-inch cookie cutter. Place on ungreased cookie sheets. Bake for 5 to 6 minutes. Cool 5 minutes before removing from pan.

Swedish Yule Cookies

OVEN TEMPERATURE: 400 degrees

YIELD: 4 dozen

1 cup (2 sticks) plus 2 tablespoons butter, softened
¾ cup sugar
1 egg
3½ cups flour

1 teaspoon baking powder
½ teaspoon salt
1 egg white, beaten
¼ teaspoon cinnamon

In large bowl, cream butter with sugar. Add egg and beat until fluffy. Sift flour with baking powder and salt. Gradually add flour mixture to butter mixture. Knead to make dough. Press into ball and wrap in plastic wrap. Refrigerate for 3 hours. Divide dough into 3 pieces. Knead each and then return 2 pieces to the refrigerator. On floured surface, roll out third piece to ⅛-inch thickness. Cut with 2½-inch round cutter. Place on cookie sheets. Repeat with remaining dough. Brush with egg white. Sprinkle with sugar and cinnamon mixture. Bake for 8 to 10 minutes. Cool for 5 minutes before removing from pan.

Ginny's Holiday Cookies

OVEN TEMPERATURE: 350 degrees   **YIELD:** 4 dozen

1 cup shortening
1½ cups sugar
3 eggs
1¼ teaspoons almond extract
4 cups flour

3 teaspoons baking powder
1 teaspoon baking soda
½ teaspoon salt
¼ cup buttermilk
¼ cup coarse sugar crystals

In large bowl, cream together shortening and sugar. Add eggs, one at a time, stirring well after each. Add almond extract. In separate bowl, sift together flour, baking powder, baking soda, and salt. Add to creamed mixture alternately with buttermilk. Mix well. Cover and refrigerate for 1 hour. On floured surface, roll dough to ¼-inch thickness. Cut out desired shapes with 2¾-inch round cookie cutter, and place on greased cookie sheets. Bake for 15 minutes or until edges begin to brown. Sprinkle with sugar. Cool for 5 minutes before removing from pan.

Swedish Christmas Cookies

OVEN TEMPERATURE: 400 degrees   **YIELD:** 5 dozen

1 cup (2 sticks) butter
¾ cup plus 2 tablespoons sugar
⅓ cup light corn syrup
½ cup almonds, chopped
½ cup candied lemon peel, chopped

4 cups flour, sifted
½ teaspoon baking soda
½ teaspoon ground cloves
1 teaspoon ground cinnamon
½ teaspoon ground ginger

In small saucepan, melt butter with sugar and corn syrup over *low* heat. Remove from heat and cool. In large bowl, stir together almonds and candied fruit. Pour butter mixture into bowl and stir well. Sift together flour, baking soda, and spices. Add to butter mixture and knead into firm dough. Divide into two rolls, wrap in plastic wrap, and refrigerate for 24 hours. Cut rolls of dough into slices ¼-inch thick. Place on greased cookie sheets 2 inches apart. Bake for 8 to 10 minutes. Cool for 5 minutes before removing from pan.

Almond Spice Cookies

OVEN TEMPERATURE: 350 degrees

YIELD: 5 dozen

4 eggs
1 cup plus 2 tablespoons sugar
3½ cups flour
½ teaspoon baking powder
1 teaspoon ground cinnamon
¼ teaspoon ground cloves

¼ teaspoon nutmeg
¼ teaspoon allspice
3½ cups almonds, ground
⅔ cup candied orange peel, chopped
1 egg yolk
1 tablespoon water

In large bowl, cream together eggs and sugar until creamy. Sift together flour, baking powder, and spices. Add almonds and candied peel. Stir egg mixture into flour mixture. On floured surface, knead to form firm dough. Divide into rolls. Wrap and refrigerate for 2 hours or overnight. Cut rolls of dough into slices ¼-inch thick. Beat egg yolk and water together and brush tops of cookies. Place on greased cookie sheets 2 inches apart. Bake for 20 minutes. Cool for 5 minutes before removing from pan.

Coconut Oats Refrigerator Cookies

OVEN TEMPERATURE: 375 degrees

YIELD: 12 dozen

1 cup (2 sticks) butter, softened
1 cup brown sugar, firmly packed
1 cup sugar
2 eggs
1½ cups flour

1 teaspoon baking soda
1 teaspoon salt
3 cups quick oats
½ cups pecans, chopped
1⅓ cups flaked coconut

In large bowl, cream butter with sugars until fluffy. Add eggs, one at a time, stirring after each. Sift together flour, baking soda, and salt. Add flour to creamed mixture and blend well. Add oats gradually, mixing well after each addition. Stir in nuts and coconut. Divide dough into thirds. Shape into rolls 2 inches wide. Wrap in plastic wrap and refrigerate for 2 hours. Let rolls stand at room temperature until soft enough to dent when pressed with finger. Cut into ⅛-inch slices. Place on ungreased cookie sheets. Bake for 10 minutes. Cool for 5 minutes before removing from pan.

Gingerbread Men

OVEN TEMPERATURE: 375 degrees **YIELD:** 8 dozen

4½ cups flour
1 teaspoon baking soda
1 teaspoon salt
1 teaspoon nutmeg

1 tablespoon ginger
1 cup shortening
1 cup sugar
1 cup molasses

Sift together flour, soda, salt, and spices. Set aside. Melt shortening in large saucepan. Add sugar and molasses and mix well. Gradually stir in about 3½ cups of flour mixture. Place on floured surface and work remaining flour mixture into dough. Wrap in plastic wrap and refrigerate for 2 hours. Roll out dough to ⅛-inch thickness. Cut into gingerbread men, using 4½-inch cutter. Place on greased cookie sheets. Bake for 6 to 8 minutes. Cool for 5 minutes before removing from pan.

Candy Cane Cookies

OVEN TEMPERATURE: 350 degrees

YIELD: 5 dozen

½ cup (1 stick) butter, softened
1¼ cups sugar
1 egg
2 teaspoons vanilla extract
3¼ cups flour

4 teaspoons baking powder
1 teaspoon salt
¼ cup milk
Red food coloring

In large bowl, cream butter with sugar. Add egg and vanilla and mix well. Sift together flour, baking powder, and salt. Add flour mixture to creamed mixture in small portions alternatively with milk. Stir until well blended. Divide dough in half. Add small amount of red coloring to half and incorporate it. Pinch off teaspoon of dough from each half. Roll each into 5-inch-long rope. Place red and plain ropes side by side. Press together lightly and twist. Bend at top. Repeat with remaining dough. Place 1 inch apart on ungreased cookie sheets. Bake for 10 minutes. Cool for 5 minutes before removing from pan.

Christmas Crescents

Oven Temperature: 375 degrees

Yield: 3 dozen

1½ cups flour
⅓ cup sugar
¼ teaspoon salt
½ cup almonds, blanched and finely grated
½ cup hazelnuts, finely grated

¾ cup (1½ sticks) plus 2 tablespoons butter
2 egg yolks
⅓ cup sugar
¼ cup powdered sugar

In large bowl, sift together flour, sugar, and salt. Add almonds and hazelnuts. Stir well. Add butter cut into small pieces and egg yolks. Knead until soft dough is formed. Form ball and wrap in plastic wrap. Refrigerate for 2 hours. Pinch off pieces of dough and roll out on floured board into pencil-thin ropes. Cut into 2-inch pieces. Curve into crescent shapes and place on cookie sheets. Bake for 10 minutes. Cool for 5 minutes before removing from pan. Mix together two remaining sugars in plastic bag or shallow dish. Toss cookies, while still warm, in sugar mixture until coated. Cool completely on parchment paper.

Caraway Cutouts

OVEN TEMPERATURE: 375 degrees   **YIELD:** 4½ dozen

½ cup (1 stick) butter, softened
1 cup sugar
2 eggs
2 cups flour

1 teaspoon baking powder
¼ teaspoon baking soda
¼ teaspoon salt
1 tablespoon caraway seeds

In large bowl, cream butter with sugar. Add eggs, one at a time, stirring after each one. In separate bowl, sift together flour, baking powder, baking soda, and salt. Stir in caraway seeds. Stir flour mixture into creamed mixture in small portions until all dry ingredients are incorporated. Divide dough in half, cover, and refrigerate for 2 hours. On floured surface, roll out dough, one portion at a time, to ⅛-inch thickness. Use cookie cutters to cut out assortment of holiday shapes. Place 2 inches apart on greased cookie sheets. Bake for 7 to 8 minutes. Cool for 5 minutes before removing from pan.

Poppy Seed Santas

OVEN TEMPERATURE: 375 degrees

YIELD: 3 to 4 dozen

¾ cup (1½ sticks) butter, softened
⅔ cup sugar
3 tablespoons honey
1 egg
2 teaspoons orange peel, finely shredded
2¼ cups flour

1 teaspoon baking powder
¼ teaspoon baking soda
1 teaspoon cinnamon
1 egg white, room temperature
1 tablespoon water
2 tablespoons poppy seeds

In large bowl, cream butter with sugar and honey. Add egg and beat until fluffy. Add orange peel. Stir. Sift together flour, baking powder, baking soda, and cinnamon. Stir into creamed mixture in small portions until incorporated. Divide dough into 2 parts. Cover and refrigerate for 2 hours. On floured surface, roll out dough, one portion at a time, to ¼-inch thickness. Use Santa cookie cutters to cut the dough. Place on greased cookie sheets, 2 inches apart. In small bowl, beat egg white with water, and brush tops of cookies. Sprinkle with poppy seeds. Bake for 8 to 10 minutes. Cool 5 minutes before removing from pan.

Cinnamon Stars

OVEN TEMPERATURE: 300 degrees   **YIELD:** 3 to 4 dozen

6 egg whites, room temperature
1 (1 pound) box powdered sugar
Grated rind of 1 lemon

1 pound unblanched almonds, finely
  grated
1 teaspoon cinnamon

Beat egg whites until stiff peaks are formed. Gradually beat in sugar until shiny pointed peaks form. Fold in lemon rind. Remove ¼ of mixture and set aside. Add almonds and cinnamon to remaining mixture, folding in just until blended. Turn out the mixture onto sugar-sprinkled surface. Roll out to ¼-inch thickness. Cut with star cookie cutter. Drop 1 teaspoon of reserved meringue on each and draw out to each point of the star. Place on lightly greased cookie sheets. Bake 40 to 50 minutes or until lightly browned and crusty. Remove from pan to parchment paper to cool.

Dark Pfefferneusse

Oven Temperature: 350 degrees

Yield: 5 dozen

Ingredients for first dough:
1¼ cups honey
¾ cup light molasses
2 tablespoons butter
½ cup shortening
1½ teaspoons cinnamon
¾ teaspoon cloves
½ teaspoon grated lemon rind, packed
6 cups flour
1½ teaspoons baking soda

Ingredients for second dough:
2 cups sugar
½ cup milk
1 egg, beaten
2½ cups flour
60 whole almonds
20 maraschino cherries, cut into quarters
½ cup powdered sugar

In heavy saucepan, combine honey, molasses, butter, shortening, cinnamon, and cloves. Bring to boil over *medium* heat. Remove from heat as soon as bubbles form. Cool slightly and stir in lemon rind. Sift half the flour with baking soda. Stir until dry ingredients are well incorporated. On floured surface, work in remainder of flour. Knead until smooth. Wrap dough tightly in several sheets of heavy waxed paper and put in warm place for 4 to 5 days. On day 5, combine sugar and milk for second dough in saucepan. Stir well over *medium* heat until mixture comes to boil. Cool. Heat to boiling again. Cool slightly and pour into bowl. Beat in egg and add flour in small portions until well incorporated. Remove first dough from waxed paper and work into second dough until well blended. On floured surface, divide dough into 3 portions. Roll out each portion to ¼-inch thickness. Cut into diamond shapes and place on baking sheets. Decorate with almonds and cherry pieces. Bake for 18 minutes. Cool for 5 minutes before removing from pan. Sprinkle with powdered sugar.

Lemon Butter Cutouts

OVEN TEMPERATURE: 350 degrees

YIELD: 2½ dozen

½ cup (1 stick) butter, softened
½ cup sugar
1 egg
1½ cups flour
½ teaspoon baking powder

2 tablespoons lemon juice
1 teaspoon lemon peel, grated
⅛ teaspoon salt
¼ cup sugar crystals

In large bowl, cream butter with sugar until smooth. Beat in egg until fluffy. Add flour, baking powder, lemon juice, lemon peel, and salt. Cover and refrigerate for 2 hours. On floured surface, roll out dough, 1 small portion at a time, to ¼-inch thickness. Use assorted 3-inch cutters to cut dough into shapes. Place on ungreased cookie sheets. Sprinkle with sugar. Bake 8 to 10 minutes. Cool 3 minutes before removing from pan to parchment paper to finish cooling.

Brandy Snaps

OVEN TEMPERATURE: 400 degrees

YIELD: 11 dozen

½ cup (1 stick) butter
1⅓ cups light brown sugar, firmly
   packed
¾ cup light corn syrup

⅛ teaspoon salt
1½ teaspoons ginger
2¾ cups flour

In heavy saucepan, combine butter, sugar, corn syrup, salt, and ginger over *low* heat. Stir until butter melts and ingredients are well blended. Remove from heat and cool slightly. Stir in flour in portions, mixing well after each until dry ingredients are completely incorporated. Wrap dough in waxed paper and refrigerate for 2 hours. Divide dough into 4 portions. On floured surface, roll out one portion at a time to a very thin $\frac{1}{16}$-inch. Cut into 2-inch rounds. Lift with spatula and place ½ inch apart on greased cookie sheets. Bake 5 minutes. Cool for 5 minutes before removing from pan.

Hungarian Christmas Crescents

OVEN TEMPERATURE: 400 degrees

YIELD: 2 dozen

2 cups flour
¼ teaspoon salt
½ cup (1 stick) butter
1 tablespoon shortening
2 egg yolks

½ cup sour cream
½ cup tart jelly
1 egg yolk, beaten
3 tablespoons milk
¼ cup powdered sugar, sifted

In large bowl, sift together flour and salt. Cut in butter and shortening with pastry blender until crumbly. Stir in egg yolks and sour cream until smooth. Shape dough into ball, wrap in waxed paper, and chill overnight. On floured surface, roll out to ⅛-inch thickness. Cut into 3-inch rounds. Place ½ teaspoon of jelly ½ inch from edge on each round. Fold the ½-inch edge over jelly until it is completely covered. Press edges to seal in jelly. Then roll up like a jelly roll and place on waxed paper with open edge on bottom. Shape into crescents. Combine egg yolk and milk. Brush cookies with mixture and place on greased cookie sheets. Bake 10 to 12 minutes. Remove to rack to cool. Sprinkle with powdered sugar.

Butter Thins

OVEN TEMPERATURE: 425 degrees

YIELD: 7 dozen

1 cup (2 sticks) butter, softened
⅔ cup sugar
1 egg
1 teaspoon vanilla extract

1 teaspoon lemon extract
2½ cups plus 1 tablespoon flour
¾ teaspoon baking powder

In large bowl, cream butter with sugar until shiny. Add egg and extracts. Beat until fluffy. In separate bowl, sift together flour and baking powder. Add to creamed mixture in portions, mixing until all dry ingredients are well incorporated. Cover and refrigerate for 1 hour. Remove ⅓ of dough at a time. On floured surface, roll out to a very thin ¹⁄₁₆-inch thickness. Cut out with 2-inch rounds and place on ungreased cookie sheets 1 inch apart. Bake for 4 to 5 minutes. Remove to rack to cool.

Ginger Crisps

OVEN TEMPERATURE: 375 degrees

YIELD: 8 to 9 dozen

½ cup (1 stick) butter
½ cup light molasses
½ cup sugar
1 tablespoon cider vinegar

2 cups flour
1½ teaspoons baking soda
1 teaspoon cinnamon
½ teaspoon ginger

In saucepan, combine butter, molasses, sugar, and vinegar. Over moderate heat, bring to boil. Boil gently for 3 minutes. Remove from heat and cool. In large bowl, sift together flour, baking soda, and spices. Add flour mixture to creamed mixture in portions, stirring well after each. Shape into ball and wrap in waxed paper. Refrigerate for 2 hours. Roll out to a very thin ⅟₁₆-inch thickness. Cut with a 2-inch round cutter. Place 1½ inches apart on greased cookie sheets. Bake for 7 minutes. Cookies should be a rich brown. Remove immediately to cake rack to cool.

Mediterranean Holiday Cookies

OVEN TEMPERATURE: 325 degrees

YIELD: 20 cookies

⅓ cup walnuts, toasted and chopped
⅓ cup golden raisins
3 tablespoons orange marmalade
2 teaspoons ground ginger
⅛ teaspoon salt
2 cups flour
1 teaspoon baking powder

1 tablespoon powdered sugar
⅛ teaspoon salt
½ cup (1 stick) plus 2 tablespoons butter
2 tablespoons canola oil
¼ cup milk
½ cup powdered sugar

Combine walnuts, raisins, marmalade, ginger, and salt in food processor. Pulse until evenly combined (1 to 2 minutes). Set aside. Sift together flour, baking powder, powdered sugar, and salt in large bowl. Add butter, oil, and milk. Combine until dough comes together. It will be damp. Roll into 20 balls. Press and pat each ball into 2½-inch round of dough. Place rounded teaspoon of filling in center of each and pull sides up around filling. Seal edges. Roll each cookie with your hands until smooth and round. Flatten cookie slightly. Place seamed-side down on parchment-lined baking sheets. Bake for 25 to 30 minutes until slightly golden. Dust with powdered sugar. Cool and dust again.

Spicy Scandinavian Cutouts

OVEN TEMPERATURE: 375 degrees   **YIELD:** 5 dozen

½ (1 stick) butter, softened
⅔ cup light brown sugar, firmly packed
2 cups flour
½ teaspoon baking soda

1½ teaspoons ground ginger
1½ teaspoons cinnamon
½ teaspoon cardamom
½ teaspoon cloves

In large bowl, cream together butter with brown sugar until fluffy. In separate bowl, sift together flour, baking soda, and spices. Gradually add flour mixture to creamed mixture until soft dough is formed. Divide into 2 parts. Wrap in plastic wrap and refrigerate for 2 hours. On floured surface, roll out dough, 1 part at a time, to a thin ⅛-inch thickness. Cut dough with assorted 3-inch cutters dipped in flour. Place cutouts 1 inch apart on greased cookie sheets. Bake 8 to 10 minutes. Cool 3 minutes before removing to parchment paper to cool completely.

Ribbon Cookies

OVEN TEMPERATURE: 375 degrees

YIELD: 9 to 10 dozen

1 cup (2 sticks) butter, softened
1¼ cups sugar
1 egg
1 teaspoon vanilla extract
2½ cups flour
1½ teaspoons baking powder

½ teaspoon salt
Red food coloring
¼ cup candied cherries, finely chopped
1 (1 ounce) square unsweetened
   chocolate, melted
1 tablespoon poppy seeds

In large bowl, cream butter with sugar. Beat in egg and vanilla. In separate bowl, sift together flour, baking powder, and salt. Add flour mixture to creamed mixture in portions. Mix until dry ingredients are incorporated. Divide dough into three equal parts. Mix a few drops red food coloring and cherries into first part. Add chocolate to second part. Add poppy seeds to third part. Line bottom of 9 x 5-inch loaf pan with waxed paper. Pack cherry mixture evenly over bottom. Cover with chocolate mixture. Cover that with poppy seed mixture. Cover with waxed paper and refrigerate overnight. Remove dough from pan and cut into thirds lengthwise. Cut horizontally into thin slices. Place on ungreased cookie sheets and bake for 12 minutes. Cool for 10 minutes before removing from pan.

Walnut Rugelach

OVEN TEMPERATURE: 350 degrees

YIELD: 45 cookies

Ingredients for dough:
1 cup (2 sticks) butter, softened
1 (8 ounce) package cream cheese, softened
½ cup sugar
1½ cups flour
¾ teaspoon salt

Ingredients for filling:
1 tablespoon butter, cut into pieces
¾ cup sugar
1 teaspoon cinnamon
⅛ teaspoon salt
1 cup walnuts, coarsely chopped
1 cup raisins, coarsely chopped
¾ cup seedless berry preserves
1 egg
1 tablespoon milk
1 teaspoon cinnamon

In large bowl, cream butter and cream cheese with sugar. In separate bowl, sift together flour and salt. Add flour mixture to creamed mixture in portions, until all dry ingredients are well incorporated. On floured surface, divide dough into 3 parts. Shape each part into ½-inch-thick rectangle. Wrap in waxed paper and refrigerate for 2 hours or until firm. For filling, cream butter with sugar. Add cinnamon and salt. Stir well. Add walnuts and raisins. Stir until well distributed. Refrigerate for 1 hour. When ready to assemble, work with 1 portion of dough at a time. On floured surface, roll out dough to 12 x 7–inch rectangle. Stir preserves in bowl and spread over dough, leaving ½-inch border on all sides. Sprinkle nut filling onto dough. Starting on long side, roll up dough. Pinch ends to seal. Wrap in waxed paper and refrigerate for 3 hours. Beat egg and milk together. In separate bowl, combine cinnamon and sugar. Unwrap 1 log at a time, and brush with egg wash. Slice log into ¾-inch slices. Roll pieces in cinnamon-sugar mixture. Place on parchment paper–lined cookie sheets 2 inches apart. Bake for 25 minutes. Cool for 5 minutes before removing from pan.

Creamy Sandwich Cookies

OVEN TEMPERATURE: 400 degrees

YIELD: 3 dozen

Ingredients for the yeast dough:
¾ cup sugar, divided
1 cup warm milk
1 package dry yeast
4 cups flour
7 tablespoons butter, melted
1 egg
½ teaspoon grated lemon rind
1 cup almonds, chopped
1 tablespoon cold milk

Ingredients for filling:
6 tablespoons butter, softened
1¼ cups powdered sugar, sifted
½ teaspoon vanilla extract

Stir ½ teaspoon of sugar into warm milk and sprinkle with yeast. Let stand until foamy (5 minutes). Stir gently to moisten any dry particles. In large bowl, sift together flour and ¼ cup of sugar. Melt 4 tablespoons of butter and cool slightly. Beat melted butter, egg, and lemon rind into yeast mixture. Add to flour mixture and work to form a soft dough. On floured surface, knead dough and spread out on cookie sheet. Cover and let rise in a warm place (1 to 1½ hours). Combine remaining butter with remaining sugar and almonds in small bowl. Add cold milk. Cool. Spread mixture over risen dough. Bake for 40 minutes to a rich golden brown. Cool on baking sheet and then cut into 1½-inch strips. Cream butter, sugar, and vanilla in small bowl until fluffy. Split each cooled strip in half horizontally. Join two strips together with cream filling.

Holiday Scripture Cookies

OVEN TEMPERATURE: 400 degrees

YIELD: 4½ dozen

Ingredients for dough:
2 cups (4 sticks) butter, softened
1 cup sugar
6 cups flour

Ingredients for icing:
3 egg whites, room temperature
½ teaspoon cream of tartar
1 (16 ounce) box powdered sugar
Red and green food coloring

In large bowl, cream butter with sugar, beating until fluffy. Add flour to creamed mixture in portions. Dough will be dry. Divide dough into 5 to 6 smaller, more manageable parts. Working with one part of dough at a time, roll out floured surface to ⅛-inch thickness. Be sure to flour rolling pin. Cut dough using 2½-inch donut cutter. Reserve center to reuse. Place cookies on ungreased cookie sheets and bake for 5 to 7 minutes or until lightly browned. Watch carefully. These burn easily. Write Christmassy-themed scripture selections on 54 (4 x 1–inch) strips of paper. Fold each one in half lengthwise, and set aside. Prepare icing by combining egg whites and cream of tartar in large bowl. Beat at *medium* speed with mixer until frothy. Gradually add sugar and continue to beat for 5 to 7 minutes. Divide into parts and add food coloring. When cookies are cool, put strip of icing at top and bottom of back side of half the cookies. Place scriptures across centers of cookies, not touching icing. Top with remainder of cookies, top side up. Decorate with icing.

Simple Sugar Cookies

OVEN TEMPERATURE: 400 degrees

YIELD: 4 dozen

1 cup shortening
1½ cups sugar
3 eggs

4 cups flour
1 teaspoon baking soda
⅛ teaspoon salt

In large bowl, cream together shortening and sugar until fluffy. Add eggs, one at a time, blending well after each. In separate bowl, sift together flour, baking soda, and salt. Add to creamed mixture in small portions, stirring well after each, until dry ingredients have been incorporated. Divide dough into 2 parts and chill for 1 hour. Chill rolling pin for 5 minutes. On floured surface, roll out dough, 1 part at a time. Dip assorted cookie cutters in sugar and press into dough. Place on ungreased cookie sheets and bake for 8 to 10 minutes or until golden brown. Cool for 5 minutes before removing from pan.

Festive Medallion Cookies

OVEN TEMPERATURE: 400 degrees

YIELD: 6 dozen

¾ cup (1½ sticks) butter, softened
1½ cups sugar
2 eggs, unbeaten
1 teaspoon vanilla extract
3⅔ cups flour
2½ teaspoons baking powder

½ teaspoon salt
4 teaspoons milk
1 (16 ounce) can vanilla butter cream
  frosting
Red and green food coloring
Silver sprinkles

In large bowl, cream butter with sugar. Add eggs, one at a time, beating after each addition. Add vanilla. Mix well. Sift together flour, baking powder, and salt. Add flour mixture alternately with milk, mixing well after each addition. Form into ball. Chill overnight. Roll to ½-inch thickness and cut with floured 3-inch scalloped cutter. Place on greased cookie sheets. Bake for 9 minutes. Cool for 5 minutes before removing from pan. Cool thoroughly on wire rack. Divide frosting in half and add 1 drop food color to each half. Frost cookies and add sprinkles.

Dutch Christmas Cookies

OVEN TEMPERATURE: 375 degrees

YIELD: 3 dozen

1 cup (2 sticks) plus 2 tablespoons butter, softened
¾ cup sugar
½ teaspoon salt
4 egg yolks
1¼ cup flour

¾ cup cornstarch
½ teaspoon baking powder
1 teaspoon rum extract
⅓ cup unsweetened cocoa powder, sifted
3 tablespoons coarse sugar

In large bowl, cream butter, sugar, and salt until fluffy. Add egg yolks one at a time, beating until smooth after each. Sift together flour, cornstarch, and baking powder. Fold into butter mixture. Knead to firm dough. Break into 2 equal parts. To the first add rum extract and knead well. Add cocoa powder to other half and knead well. Wrap separately in plastic wrap and refrigerate for 1 hour. On floured surface, roll out light and dark dough separately into a rectangular shape of about ¹⁄₁₆-inch thickness. Place half the dark dough on top of half the light dough. Repeat, forming 4 alternating layers. Press together and cut into small oblongs. Sprinkle with sugar and place on greased cookie sheets. Bake for 15 to 20 minutes. Cool for 5 minutes before removing from pan.

Almond Hearts

OVEN TEMPERATURE: 400 degrees

YIELD: 3 dozen

1 cup (2 sticks) plus 2 tablespoons
  butter, softened
1 cup powdered sugar, sifted

2 egg yolks
1 cup almonds, ground
3 cups flour, sifted

In large bowl, cream butter with sugar. Add 1 egg yolk and beat until creamy.
Add ground almonds and flour. Knead quickly to firm dough and refrigerate
for 2 hours. On floured surface, roll out dough to ¼-inch thickness. Cut into
heart shapes. Place on ungreased cookie sheets. Beat second egg yolk and brush
tops of cookies with it. Bake for 10 to 12 minutes. Cool for 5 minutes before
removing from pan.

Norwegian Christmas Rings

OVEN TEMPERATURE: 375 degrees

YIELD: 3 dozen

3 eggs
1 egg yolk
1¼ cups powdered sugar
1 cup (2 sticks) plus 1 tablespoon
    butter, softened

1 teaspoon vanilla extract
2¼ cups flour
1 egg yolk, beaten
1 teaspoon coarse sugar

Boil 3 eggs for 10 to 12 minutes. Remove from heat and place in cold water. When cooled, peel and press through a strainer. Add egg yolk and sugar. Add butter and vanilla and work together until well blended. Add flour and knead to form soft dough. Press into ball and wrap in plastic wrap. Refrigerate for 3 hours. On floured board, pinch off pieces of dough, enough to form a piece about 4 inches long and ¼ inch wide. Brush ends with beaten egg yolk and press together to form rings. Brush with beaten egg yolk and sprinkle with sugar. Place on cookie sheets and bake for 10 to 12 minutes. Cool for 5 minutes before removing from pan.

Nutmeg Cookies

OVEN TEMPERATURE: 400 degrees

YIELD: 3 dozen

½ cup (1 stick) butter, softened
½ cup sugar
1 egg
Peel of ½ lemon, grated
¼ teaspoon ground nutmeg

1 cup flour, sifted
1 cup hazelnuts, finely chopped
2 cups white bread crumbs
1 egg yolk, beaten

In medium bowl, cream butter and sugar. Add egg, lemon peel, and nutmeg. Stir until well blended. Combine flour, hazelnuts, and bread crumbs. Mix well. Add to butter mixture. Knead to form soft dough. Press into ball and wrap in plastic wrap. Refrigerate for 2 hours. On floured surface, roll out dough to ¼-inch thickness. Cut out small scalloped arcs about 2½ inches long and 1 inch wide. Place on cookie sheets and brush with egg yolk. Bake for 10 to 15 minutes. Cool for 5 minutes before removing from pan.

Notes

Notes

Notes

Notes

Notes

Notes

Notes

Notes

Index

Rejoice greatly, O daughter of Zion! Shout,
O daughter of Jerusalem! Behold your King is coming
to you; He is just and having salvation, lowly and
riding on a donkey, a colt, the foal of a donkey.

ZECHARIAH 9:9